MYP English

Language Acquisition

A concept-based approach

Phase

3

Kevin Morley
and Alexei Gafan

OXFORD

OXFORD
UNIVERSITY PRESS

Great Clarendon Street, Oxford, OX2 6DP, United Kingdom

Oxford University Press is a department of the University of Oxford. It furthers the University's objective of excellence in research, scholarship, and education by publishing worldwide. Oxford is a registered trade mark of Oxford University Press in the UK and in certain other countries

British Library Cataloguing in Publication Data

Data available

978-0-19-839802-8

10 9 8 7 6 5 4 3 2

Paper used in the production of this book is a natural, recyclable product made from wood grown in sustainable forests. The manufacturing process conforms to the environmental regulations of the country of origin.

Printed in India by Multivista Global Pvt. Ltd

Acknowledgements

The publisher and authors would like to thank the following for permission to use photographs and other copyright material:

Cover: Florian Meissner/EyeEm/Getty Images; **p2, 8, 20, 22, 27, 35, 36, 38, 40, 45, 47, 49, 53, 55, 59, 76, 79(t), 89, 92, 94, 99(b), 105(b), 107, 108, 118, 119, 120, 121(t), 144, 149, 155, 156, 158, 161, 162, 163(r), 168, 173, 175, 191, 208, 216, 223, 229:** © Shutterstock; **p3:** Thinkstock; **p6:** Betsie Van der Meer/Stone/Getty Images; **p13:** iStockphoto; **p14:** Photodisc/Getty Images; **p16:** OUP; **p18:** Radius Images/Alamy Stock Photo; **p21:** OUP; **p28:** Shutterstock/OUP; **p31:** iStockphoto; **p37:** OUP; **p44:** Ian Shaw/Alamy Stock Photo; **p50:** Dennis Kitchen Studio, Inc; **p52:** OUP; **p57(t):** Stephen Derr/The Image Bank/Getty Images; **p57(b):** Lemonlight features/Alamy Stock Photo; **p63:** Juice Images; **p65:** Photodisc/Getty Images/Oxford University Press; **p69:** iStockphoto; **p71(l):** paul prescott/Shutterstock; **p71(tr):** SONNY TUMBELAKA/Getty Images; **p71(tm):** paul prescott/Shutterstock; **p71(bm):** paul prescott/Shutterstock; **p71(br):** paul prescott/Shutterstock; **p74:** Learning Fundamentals; **p77:** Hero Images Inc./Alamy Stock Photo; **p78:** World History Archive/Alamy Stock Photo; **p79(b):** Wikimedia Commons/Public Domain; **p85:** Granger Historical Picture Archive/Alamy Stock Photo; **p86:** iStockphoto; **p87(t):** Peter M Corr/Alamy Stock Photo; **p87(b):** iStockphoto; **p90:** iStockphoto; **p91:** Fuse/Corbis/Getty Images; **p93:** Keren Su/China Span/Alamy Stock Photo; **p98:** John Springer Collection/Contributor/Corbis Historical/Getty Images; **p99(t):** 1MoreCreative/E+/Getty Images; **p100:** Tetra Images/Alamy Stock Photo; **p101:** Corel; **p104:** JPagetRFphotos/Alamy Stock Photo; **p105:** Chronicle/Alamy Stock Photo; **p105(t):** Bob Daemmrich/Alamy Stock Photo; **p111:** Purestock; **p114:** Shutterstock/OUP; **p116:** Chronicle/Alamy Stock Photo; **p121(b):** Edgardo Contreras/DigitalVision/Getty Images; **p123:** George Gojkovich/Getty Images; **p126:** Radius Images; **p127:** I Beat the Odds, Michael Oher, 2012/Reproduced by permission of Penguin Random House; **p128:** Adams Picture Library; **p133:** Kraig Lieb/Alamy Stock Photo; **p134:** Corbis; **p135(t):** Ecelop/Dreamstime; **p135(ml):** OUP; **p137:** Everett Collection, Inc./Alamy Stock Photo; **p138:** Agencja Fotograficzna Caro/Alamy Stock Photo; **p139:** Michael de Adder; **p143:** Digital Vision/Peter Mason; **p147:** kmt_rf; **p151:** BEBETO MATTHEWS/REX/Shutterstock; **p163(l):** iStockphoto; **p165:** Stockbroker/MBI/Alamy Stock Photo; **p167:** CAROL & MIKE WERNER/VISUALS UNLIMITED, INC./SCIENCE PHOTO LIBRARY; **p169(l):** OUP; **p169(r):** Sellingpix/Dreamstime; **p170:** Grant Snider; **p171:** Shutterstock/OUP; **p176:** INSADCO Photography; **p180:** Shutterstock/OUP; **p185:** iStockphoto; **p187:** OUP; **p189:** guteksk7/Shutterstock; **p190:** TaylorHerring; **p194:** RooM the Agency Mobile/Alamy Stock Photo; **p195:** Theodor Kittelsen [Public domain], via Wikimedia Commons; **p197:** Blend Images; **p198:** iStockphoto; **p203:** Gareth Boden; **p205:** Baloo/jantoo.com/Cartoonstock; **p207:** Image Source; **p209, 230:** Getty Images/Comstock; **p212(t):** ColorBlind Images/Blend Images; **p212(m):** Richard Lewisohn/Image Source; **p212(b):** Chris King; **p215(tl):** ITAR-TASS Photo Agency/Alamy Stock Photo; **p215(tr):** Moviestore Collection/REX/Shutterstock; **p215(bl):** Collection Christophel/Alamy Stock Photo; **p215(br):** Photo 12/Alamy Stock Photo; **p220:** iStockphoto; **p226:** Courtesy of FranklinFilmmakers; **p231:** PhotosIndia.com LLC/Alamy Stock Photo.

Artwork by Aptara Inc.

Every effort has been made to contact copyright holders of material reproduced in this book. Any omissions will be rectified in subsequent printings if notice is given to the publisher.

We are grateful to the authors and publishers for use of extracts from their titles and in particular for the following:

'Blind men and an elephant' from http://www.peacecorps.gov. Reproduced by permission

C. George Boeree: 'Maslow's Hierarchy of Needs' from http://www.ship.edu/~cgboeree/maslow.html. Copyright 1998, 2006 by C. George Boeree. Reproduced by permission.

Vyvyan Evans, (Professor of Linguistics, Bangor University): 'No the rise of the emoji doesn't spell the end of language' May 22, 2015 from http://theconversation.com. Reproduced by permission.

Judith H. Katz: *White Awareness: Handbook for Anti-Racism Training*, University of Oklahoma Press, 1978. Republished with permission of University of Oklahoma Press; permission conveyed through Copyright Clearance Center, Inc.

'How to make friends easily if you're a teen' from http://www.wikihow.com/Make-Friends-Easily-if-You're-a-Teen. Article provided by wikiHow. The material is licensed under a Creative Commons license, http://creativecommons.org/licenses/by-nc-sa/3.0/.

D'Arcy Lyness: 'Moving to Middle School' from http://kidshealth.org © The Nemours Foundation/KidsHealth. Reproduced by permission.

'Making a difference' from http://www.canadianfeedthechildren.ca. Reproduced by permission.

Seema Mody: 'Emojis: The Death of the Written Language' from http://www.cnbc.com. Courtesy of CNBC.

Liz Murray: 'My parents were desperate drug addicts. I'm a Harvard graduate'. https://www.theguardian.com. Copyright Guardian News & Media Ltd 2017.

'The Story of Michael Oher' from http://www.oprah.com. Excerpt courtesy of Oprah.com.

'How to make friends easily if you're a teen' from http://www.wikihow.com/Make-Friends-Easily-if-You're-a-Teen. Article provided by wikiHow. The material is available under a Creative Commons license, http://creativecommons.org/licenses/by-nc-sa/3.0/.

'What is Waste' from http://aries.mq.edu.au. Reproduced by permission of The Co-operators.

D'Arcy Lyness: 'Moving to Middle School' from http://kidshealth.org © The Nemours Foundation/KidsHealth. Reproduced by permission.

We have made every effort to trace and contact all copyright holders before publication, but if notified of any errors or omissions, the publisher will be happy to rectify these at the earliest opportunity.

Introduction

Teachers

This textbook has been written specifically for teachers and students of the IB MYP English Language Acquisition Phase 3 course as a series of six stand-alone MYP units.

Each chapter focuses on a different statement of inquiry, based on a key concept, related concepts and a global context. The chapters are written to systematically support students as they explore the Statement of Inquiry through a series of factual, conceptual and debatable questions. Each chapter focuses on the specific objectives of the Language Acquisition course and includes formative and summative assessments that cover the four grading criteria.

We have focused our formative and summative tasks on the writing of different text types, for different purposes and audiences. Students learn about the form and function of text types by first reading real and engaging examples of texts: oral, visual and written. We have also provided writing activities that enable the students to learn the conventions of text types and support them in producing their own authentic texts. The teaching of particular parts of language and grammar is a decision for you, as a teacher, to make, depending on the requirements of your curriculum.

To help ensure that you cover all the learning objectives and are able to assess all the strands of the grading criteria at least twice in a year, we have designed units that cover three or more of the four learning objectives per unit, including comprehension of spoken and visual text, comprehension of written and visual text, communicating in response to spoken and/or written and/or visual text, and using language in a spoken and/or written form. We have added the number "3" to the criteria purely to point out that they relate to Phase 3.

The structure of each unit provides teachers and students with plenty of formative assessment opportunities to help make sure that learning is taking place and that the inquiry, concepts and contexts are well understood. To further assist you with this, we have provided downloadable worksheets which provide you and your students with the opportunity to download and complete the tasks in the textbook. These include useful planning and scaffolding sections which will help your students learn how to plan and structure their written and oral tasks. The summative assessments in this book build on the formative tasks in the chapter and allow students to demonstrate their own understanding of the concepts covered in the unit, as well as provide students with authentic and contextualized opportunities to produce personal, authentic and challenging responses to the research questions.

An exciting development in the latest iteration of the MYP is the inclusion of action and service. It is expected that student engagement in authentic topics will lead them to want to take action, by exploring a topic further or by taking action as service. We have written and designed each chapter to include issues that will be of interest and concern to teenagers. At the end of each chapter we provide you and your students with suggested action and service activities, as well as further suggestions of spoken, visual and written texts that you may wish to explore.

Students

As a student of IB MYP English Language Acquisition Phase 3, you have been provided with a range of issues, topics and texts in this book that will enable you to further develop your understanding and use of English, while giving you the opportunity to engage with real issues and debates. The aim of this book is to give you the skills necessary to create your own answers and to develop your own responses to the conceptual and debateable questions in each chapter.

The activities in the chapters will help you to understand the Key and Related Concepts covered in each chapter. You will get to practise your reading, writing, speaking and listening skills before your final assessment at the end of each chapter. Working through the tasks and questions will help you prepare for the summative (final) activities by providing you with many opportunities to think about issues, plan responses and practice writing and speaking for different purposes. Our aim is that you will have the skills necessary to express your own thoughts and opinions on the issues and topics covered in this book. If you are inspired by a topic and would like to learn more about an issue or use your communication skills to help others, we have included a section at the end of each chapter with suggestions for action and service that you can engage in. Of course, these are just ideas – you can add and improve them to make them more personal and meaningful.

Since many of the tasks and activities ask you to answer questions and fill out tables or forms, these have been provided for you as downloadable worksheets. Instead of writing your answers in this book, you can print out the worksheets and answer the questions on paper or choose to write the answers on your computer and share your thoughts and answers with your teachers and classmates. Visit the website to download these:

www.oxfordsecondary.co.uk/9780198398028

When writing this book, we have chosen texts from different parts of the world, to ensure that you are given an international outlook on the issues and topics you will be studying. We have chosen certain written and visual texts for you to study and have included a number of suggestions of other texts. However, we are aware that you will have your own suggestions and ideas about what you would like to read, watch and listen to. The final assessments in this book have been designed to encourage you to find and engage with texts of your own choosing. Feel free to use our ideas as suggestions, and to talk to your teacher about what you would like to read, watch and listen to. That's the great thing about being an MYP student – your views, ideas and suggestions are important!

Approaches to learning (ATLs)

Most textbooks teach you what to learn. This student book can also help you to learn how to become a better learner by helping you to develop a variety of "Approaches to learning" or "ATL", for short.

These ATLs encompass the skills you need to achieve success in English Language Acquisition. In this book you will receive a great deal of practical advice and practice opportunities for listening, speaking, reading and writing in English. Moreover, ATLs are also cross-curricular. This means you can easily use the skills you learn in English Language Acquisition in other subjects within the MYP.

There are five broad categories of ATL skills you will learn to use in this book:

- Thinking skills
- Communication skills
- Social skills
- Research skills
- Self-management skills

Beyond the MYP, these ATL skills also will enable you to prepare for further success in the IB Diploma Programme, or the IB Career Related Certificate. Ultimately, ATLs can help you to develop the transferable learning skills that you will need for college, work and life in the 21st century. They will allow you to participate fully in local, national and global communities.

The authors have signposted specific ATL activities at various stages of each inquiry-based unit. Here is an example:

> **ATL Communication and thinking skills**
>
> What are the facts here? In order to answer the question you must:
>
> - gather relevant information to formulate an argument
> - recognize unstated bias
> - draw reasonable conclusions and generalizations
> - revise understanding based on new information and evidence.

These ATL activities help you to improve how you learn. In this way, you can practice and improve these skills in preparation for the summative assessments at the end of each chapter.

Below, you will find a list of all the ATLs illustrated in the book. The list also allows you to identify, articulate and reflect on the specific ATLs you are using at any particular moment. You can use this inventory as a checklist in order to identify new skills you may wish to develop.

A. Communication skills

COMMUNICATING THROUGH INTERACTION
- Interpret and use effectively modes of non-verbal communication
- Use a variety of speaking techniques to communicate with a variety of audiences
- Use appropriate forms of writing for different purposes and audiences
- Use a variety of media to communicate with a range of audiences
- Negotiate ideas and knowledge with peers and teachers
- Participate in, and contribute to, digital social media networks
- Collaborate with peers and experts using a variety of digital environments and media
- Share ideas with multiple audiences using a variety of digital environments and media

COMMUNICATING THROUGH LANGUAGE ACTIVITIES
- Preview and skim texts to build understanding
- Read critically and for comprehension
- Read a variety of sources for information and for pleasure
- Make inferences and draw conclusions
- Paraphrase accurately and concisely
- Take effective notes in class
- Make effective summary notes for studying
- Use a variety of organizers for academic writing tasks
- Use and interpret a range of discipline-specific terms and symbols
- Write for different purposes
- Organize and depict information logically
- Structure information into summaries and reports

B. Social skill

COLLABORATIVE SKILLS
- Practise empathy
- Listen actively to other perspectives and ideas
- Encourage others to contribute
- Delegate and share responsibility for decision-making
- Help others to succeed
- Take responsibility for one's own actions
- Manage and resolve conflict, and work collaboratively in teams
- Build consensus
- Make fair and equitable decisions
- Negotiate effectively
- Exercise leadership and take on a variety of roles within groups
- Give and receive meaningful feedback
- Advocate for one's own rights and needs

C. Self-management skills

ORGANIZATION SKILLS

- Manage time and tasks effectively
- Plan short- and long-term assignments; meet deadlines
- Create plans to prepare for summative assessments (examinations and performances)
- Keep and use a weekly planner for assignments
- Set goals that are challenging and realistic
- Plan strategies and take action to achieve personal and academic goals
- Use appropriate strategies for organizing complex information
- Understand and use sensory learning preferences (learning styles)

D. Research skills

INFORMATION LITERACY SKILLS

- Find, interpret and judge information
- Collect, record and verify data
- Access information to be informed and inform others
- Make connections between various sources of information
- Create new information
- Present information in a variety of formats and platforms
- Collect and analyse data to identify solutions and make informed decisions
- Process data and report results
- Use critical-literacy skills to analyse and interpret media communications

MEDIA LITERACY SKILLS

- Interact with media to use and create ideas and information
- Locate, organize, analyse, evaluate, synthesize and ethically use information from a variety of sources and media
- Make informed choices about personal viewing experiences
- Understand the impact of media representations and modes of presentation
- Seek a range of perspectives from multiple and varied sources
- Communicate information and ideas effectively to multiple audiences using a variety of media and formats

E. Thinking skills

CRITICAL THINKING SKILLS

- Analyse and evaluate issues and ideas
- Gather and organize relevant information to formulate an argument
- Interpret data
- Evaluate evidence and arguments
- Draw reasonable conclusions and generalizations
- Test generalizations and conclusions
- Revise understanding based on new information and evidence
- Consider ideas from multiple perspectives
- Develop contrary or opposing arguments
- Propose and evaluate a variety of solutions
- Identify obstacles and challenges
- Use models and simulations to explore complex systems and issues
- Identify trends and forecast possibilities

CREATIVE THINKING SKILLS

- Generate novel ideas and consider new perspectives
- Use brainstorming and visual diagrams to generate new ideas and inquiries
- Consider multiple alternatives
- Create novel solutions to authentic problems
- Make unexpected or unusual connections between objects and/or ideas
- Make guesses, ask "what if" questions and generate testable hypotheses
- Apply existing knowledge to generate new ideas, products or processes
- Create original works and ideas; use existing works and ideas in new ways
- Practise visible thinking strategies and techniques
- Generate metaphors and analogies

TRANSFER SKILLS

- Use skills and knowledge in multiple contexts
- Make connections between subject groups and disciplines
- Apply skills and knowledge in situations beyond the classroom

Contents

1 Friendship

In context

Global context: Identities and relationships

In this chapter you will explore questions related to friendship. In turn this will require you to think about human relationships and related topics such as identity – who you are; your beliefs and values; your mental, social and spiritual health; in short, what it means to be human. All students of Language Acquisition understand that learning a language involves learning to interact with another culture whose customs may be different from your own, or the one that you are used to. Making new friendships requires us to step outside our comfort zones.

Key concept: Culture

Culture is a range of learned and shared beliefs, values, interests, attitudes, products, ways of knowing and patterns of behaviour created by human communities. The concept of culture is dynamic and organic. Learning the language of a community provides opportunities to embrace diversity, to interact with others with sensitivity and empathy, and to participate in meaningful interactions, which may lead to new friendships. These intercultural friendships allow us to develop new intercultural competences and awareness. We are able to develop international-mindedness and ultimately to become global citizens.

Related concept: Meaning

What is communicated, by intention or by implication, using any range of human expression. It is sometimes referred to as "message". Meaning includes "layers of meaning", nuance, denotation, connotation, inference, subtext.

Statement of inquiry

Language is an essential tool that helps us to understand, reflect on and develop close personal, social and cultural friendships in local and global contexts.

Inquiry questions

→ What happens to you when you start at a new school?

→ How can you make friends in a new school?

→ Why can international students sometimes find it hard to make friends?

→ What and how does the audio-visual text communicate about the theme of "Making friends"?

→ To what extent should it be the responsibility of teachers and students to make new students welcome?

→ How should you act, and what should you say, to make new friends at a new school?

What happens to you when you start at a new school?

Factual question

Before you read Text A

Criterion 3Ci

What do you know about friendship? Before you begin this chapter, conduct a class brainstorming session. You could start by finding as many ways as possible to finish these sentences:

"Good friends always …" "Good friends never …"

Focusing activity

Look at the girl in the picture. It is her first day in a new school. What do you imagine she is thinking? What is she feeling? What advice would you give her to make a success of her first day?

Now read Text A.

Diary entries: A new school

Natasha is going to be a new student at your school. She has come from an international school in Europe and she is still learning English.

She is rather shy and frightened at the thought of her new school and her new surroundings. She writes a series of diary entries about this.

Text A

Thursday 9th

Dear diary,

I'm going into 9th grade next week. All of my friends are going back to my old school in a different country and I'll have no friends... I am very shy around people I don't know. So it's kind of hard for me to make new friends... But I really want to.

And I'm really nervous about the first day because I won't have anyone to sit with at lunch or anything. And I'm worried that everyone will have their friends from school... and at lunch they will probably all sit with their old friends... I'm really nervous...

I hate it when I go to a new school and I'm all alone and don't know anyone and everyone else is talking to all their friends... I'm hoping they won't have too many classes with their friends so I won't be the only one who doesn't know anyone...

Sunday 12th

Dear diary

I realise it's natural for me to feel a bit afraid about starting a new school. New places are scary; even my mum and dad are feeling anxious because they are starting new jobs in a new country. I keep telling myself that feeling nervous is perfectly understandable.

I feel like I've stepped into one of those teen movies. You know, the ones where I'm the geeky girl no one talks to. I'm not surprised I am having bad dreams about getting lost in the halls or having no one to eat lunch with.

I need to take a deep breath and relax. First, it's important to remember I'm not alone. Everyone is nervous about starting a new school. I have to remember that life is filled with new adventures; new schools and new friends are part of the journey! I can make the adventure less stressful by figuring out where to fit in. I know I'll miss all my really good friends but I am sure I'll meet some great new people.

Tuesday 14th

Dear diary,

I've found the address of an Internet forum I can visit to see what advice they can offer kids like me, who are moving to a new school in a new country. The trouble is I feel very nervous about letting other people know how insecure I feel. Still, nothing ventured, nothing gained, as British people say, apparently.

Text handling – Factual assessment of Text A

Criterion 3Bi

1 Multiple-choice questions

1. Natasha is moving to a new school:
   A. in the same town
   B. in a different part of the same country
   C. that is an international school in her country
   D. in a new country.

2. What worries Natasha most is:
   A. not having friends
   B. learning new subjects
   C. having new teachers
   D. being in a new country.

3. She also worries about being:
   A. hungry   C. bullied
   B. nervous   D. lonely.

4. In paragraph three of her diary she hopes that:
   A. she will be the only new student in Grade 9
   B. she will enjoy her new classes in Grade 9
   C. the students will be in different classes to Grade 8
   D. the students will be in the same classes as in Grade 8.

5. On the 12th of the month Natasha writes that:
   A. it is not normal to worry about starting something new
   B. even adults worry about starting a new job
   C. her parents are never nervous about changes
   D. nobody should worry too much about changes.

6. She says she is having bad dreams because she is afraid of:
   A. getting lost   C. being too popular
   B. having no one to talk to   D. being in a movie.

7. She ends the diary entry on the 12th by realizing:
   A. she will have a new adventure
   B. she will fit in easily
   C. she needs to take a journey
   D. she needs to learn how to take deep breaths.

2 Short-answer questions

8. On the 14th where does Natasha say she can find help?
9. Explain the meaning of the phrase: "Nothing ventured, nothing gained".
10. Overall, do you think Natasha is optimistic, pessimistic or uncertain about entering her new school?
    Justify your answer with evidence from the text.

ATL Social skills

You may wish to work on the answers in pairs. In this way you can:

- listen actively to other perspectives and ideas
- encourage others to contribute
- share responsibility for decision-making
- help others to succeed

ATL Thinking skills

Criterion 3Bi

Analysing and evaluating issues and ideas

1 Natasha starts each diary entry with the words, "Dear diary". Who is she really writing to and why is she writing?

2 Do you think it is helpful for Natasha to keep a diary? Give reasons for your answer using evidence from the text.

Formative oral and interactive skills: Role-play – Natasha's first day at school

Criteria 3Ci, 3Cii

ATL Thinking skills

Before you start reading, use your prior knowledge and creativity to answer this question: what do you already know about role plays?

Brainstorm your answers and create a list.

In a role-play a small group of students "become" different characters for a short time. The idea is to act out an imaginary scene where you put yourself in another person's situation. This way you can express ideas that may be different from your own.

While the role-play is taking place, the rest of the class can observe and judge the action. You can look at the characters' actions and decide who, if anyone, is right and who is wrong. You can maybe offer another viewpoint, or suggest an alternative ending. You can also make helpful comments on the participants' use of language.

At the end, students can come to an opinion on the action they have seen.

Role-plays are also a great way of practising your fluency in English as you have a chance to use English in new ways and situations. You also have to improvise: to use the English you know to communicate your ideas quickly and naturally. However, role-plays work best when you prepare before you start.

Make sure you have prepared the ideas and language you want to use. You may want the language on a cue card like the one below.

Now imagine what it would be like for a student like Natasha to start at your school. The student will be nervous about coming into a new school, a new culture and trying to make new friends.

Planning and scaffolding

Work in groups of three or four. In each group there should be two teams. One team will work out what questions a new student would want to ask about the school. This group could make a cue card that looks like the one here. On the cue card list all the things you would want to know about as a new student.

Ten things a new student wants to know about their new school

1.
2.
3.
4.
5.

6.
7.
8.
9.
10

Planning and scaffolding

The second team should be students already at your school: "Student A", "Student B" and "Student C". This team should think of ten things Natasha really needs to know about the school. This group could make a cue card that looks like this:

Conduct the role-play in pairs. Ensure that:

A. the new student gets answers to all ten questions

B. students A, B and C make sure the new student knows the ten things you think are important

C. the observers make notes and come to a conclusion about the success of the conversation; for example, work out whether all the new student's concerns have been answered.

> Ten important things Natasha needs to know about the school
>
> 1.   6.
>
> 2.   7.
>
> 3.   8.
>
> 4.   9.
>
> 5.   10

Planning and scaffolding   Criteria 3Ciii 3Civ

Before you conduct the role-play, decide how the new student and the other students will talk to each other:

A. formally or informally

B. politely or impolitely

C. friendly or impersonally.

Choose one adverb from each pair to describe how the different students would probably speak to each other.

1. Natasha will probably speak to the other students <u>informally</u>, _____ and _____.

2. The other students will probably speak to Natasha _____, _____ and _____.

3. The other students will probably speak to each other _____ _____ and _____.

Formative written activity: Controlled writing in response to Text A

Natasha arrives at your school. She meets you and your friends on her first day. Write Natasha's diary entry for that day. You should write between 200 and 250 words. Give your work a title.

Before you write

It is a good idea to plan your ideas before you write. You can use the table to help your writing. Look at the examples in Text A above.

Structure	Beginning/opening: Dear diary, Middle: what happened Ending: your thoughts about your first day
Content	Think about: How was Natasha feeling on her first day? How did the first meeting go? What were Natasha's first impressions of you and your friends?
Language and audience	You are writing in the first person: "I". Write about events that have finished in the simple past. How will you write to yourself? a. formally or informally b. personally or impersonally

Conclusion to the factual question

What happens to you when you start at a new school?

Having examined this section, what is your answer to the factual question?

How do you make friends in a new school?

Discussion and debate

Criteria 3Cii, 3Ciii

When Natasha went to the Internet forum she received plenty of advice from different people.

In groups, rate each piece of advice from 1 to 5, where 1 is not very good and 5 is excellent. Next come up with your own additional list of ideas for "How to survive the first week at our school as a new student". When you have finished, compare your list with another student's list. Make a list of the best five pieces of advice you can offer a student new to you school.

Advice	Your rating
In class ask someone for help with your work.	
Answer as many of the teacher's questions as you can.	
If someone looks at you, smile at him or her.	
Join lots of after-school clubs or sports teams.	
Find one person in your class who seems nice and friendly.	
Make friends with any other new students in Grade 9.	
Say to someone, "I'm new and don't know anyone. Can I go to classes with you for the day?"	
Talk to people before the end of each period/class.	
Tell everyone about your own country.	
Never wait for people to talk to you.	

Before you read Text B

Criterion 3Bi

In the text below there are seven paragraphs, each giving a different piece of advice.

Ten headings are listed below. Which do you think are the best seven pieces of advice to give to a new student? Make your own personal list. Show it to a partner. Decide whose list is better. Give reasons for your answers.

- Be a good listener
- Don't try too hard
- Smile a lot
- Be yourself
- Make the first move
- Develop friendships
- Do team sports
- Relax
- Be nice
- Include new friends in your life

ATL Research skills

How do you decide what is good advice? Use these skills to complete the task opposite.

- Interpret and judge information.
- Make connections between various. sources of information
- Create new information.
- Present information in a new format.
- Identify solutions and make informed decisions.
- Report results.

Text B

How to make friends easily if you're a teen

A.

It's all about confidence – if you are nervous or try too hard to look cool, you won't make many friends. You have to think of good reasons why someone would like to meet you, think of the good points you have.

B.

Don't be shy and wait for people to talk to you. It won't help you in anything. Look around for someone that seems interesting, then go up to talk to him or her. Say hello, give them your name if they don't know your name already, ask how they are and just talk to them.

C.

It is very helpful if you try to find out what you and the person you are trying to befriend have in common. Don't look too serious. Be friendly and cheerful. How do you expect them to like you if you are not friendly?

D.

Give attention to what people say, look straight in their eyes and show you're paying attention. Nod, agree, show you find what they're saying is interesting. It's important to be a good listener. If this new person feels like you're listening to them, your new friend will enjoy your company more.

E.

I know you've heard it a lot of times, but no one really likes a fake person that no one really knows. Don't pretend and say things you don't mean. Be natural and you will get people that like you for being you.

F.

You may talk to someone now but soon they'll forget you. Take time to say "Hi" to new people every day. Ask how they are doing. When you greet them, say things like, "Hey Alex!", "What you doing, Sarah?", "What's up, Miranda?" If you do that every day, they'll be happy that you remembered them.

G.

Invite your new friends to go out together with you, go to the mall or hang out at a cool place. You guys can have fun together. Build your social circle from there.

Adapted from http://www.wikihow.com/
Make-Friends-Easily-if-You're-a-Teen

Text handling – Factual meaning of Text B

1 Matching parts of a text

Match the headings 1–10 to the paragraphs A–G. There are more headings than paragraphs.

1. Be a good listener
2. Don't try too hard
3. Smile a lot
4. Be yourself
5. Make the first move
6. Develop friendships
7. Do team sports
8. Relax
9. Be nice
10. Include new friends in your life

2 Multiple-choice questions

Choose the correct answer from A, B, C, or D.

1. In paragraph A the writer says that in order to make friends the most important thing is to:
    A. look cool
    B. meet people
    C. be confident
    D. think of your positive qualities. ☐

2. In paragraph B the writer says that the best thing is to:
    A. say your name
    B. say something interesting
    C. wait for people to talk to you
    D. talk to new people. ☐

3. In paragraph C the writer says that you should try to be:
    A. helpful
    B. friendly
    C. serious
    D. caring. ☐

4. In paragraph D the writer says that when talking to someone new you should:
    A. enjoy the person's company
    B. look the person in the eye
    C. pay attention
    D. nod and agree. ☐

5. In paragraph E the writer says that the worst thing to do is to:
    A. be false
    B. say what you mean
    C. pretend to like someone
    D. be mean. ☐

6. In paragraph F the writer says people will remember you if you:
    A. are happy
    B. know their names
    C. ask them questions
    D. are a new friend. ☐

7. In paragraph G the writer says you can also make new friends by:
    A. meeting them at clubs
    B. inviting them home
    C. inviting them to hang out outside school
    D. inviting them to hang out inside school. ☐

Formative oral and interactive skills: Role-play

Planning and scaffolding

Your English class organizes a "getting to know you" session for all new students. Imagine you are a new student from another country. Invent a completely new identity for yourself. Fill in the student information sheet below to create this new identity. You will use this as a cue card later.

Student Information Sheet

Personal facts

Last name _ _ _ _ _ _ _ _ _ _ _ _ First name _ _ _ _ _ _ _ _ _ _ Middle name _ _ _ _ _ _ _ _

Preferred name/nickname _

Birthday _

Parents' names _

Parents' jobs _

Siblings (names and ages) _

Home country _

Home city _

Previous school _

My likes and dislikes

I love (list three) _ .

I hate (list three) _ .

The farthest I have ever travelled from home is _ .

My favourite place in the world is _ .

The person I admire is _ because

_ _

The best movie I've ever seen was _ because

_ _

My favourite kind of music is _

My favourite sport is _

My extra-curricular activities and hobbies are _

I worry about _ .

I'm curious about _ .

Five years from now I hope to be _ .

Work in pairs. Imagine you are both new students from other countries. Ask and answer questions to get to know as much as you can about the other person. Use a copy of the student information sheet for your answers and to help you formulate questions for your partner.

Before you conduct the role-play, decide how the new student and the other students will talk to each other:

A. formally or informally

B. politely or impolitely

C. friendly or impersonally.

Formative writing activity: Diary
Criterion 3Di

A couple of days before the start of term in her new school, Natasha received three more pieces of advice on the Internet forum. How would Natasha react to this advice? Write Natasha's diary entry. Write between 200 and 250 words.

> "Honestly, I think the first days of school are crazy. Everyone is lost. Everyone will be walking around looking for their friends, or looking for their next classes. I am telling you that there are going to be more students like you, who don't have any of their friends there. So don't worry." Youji

> "Teachers usually will make you all introduce yourself and maybe you should say you're new and you would like to make friends because none of your friends go to your new school. It's OK to ask whether anyone has any advice. Don't be nervous, seriously it's not as bad as it seems." Fabio

> "You'll have both good and bad times. It's when you'll learn about who you are and what you want to do in life. Expect people to be very different to you. Expect to find some really generous people and some really immature kids. Just look for people who you feel comfortable with and I think you'll have a great year at school." Stella

Planning and scaffolding   Criteria 3Dii, 3Diii

Use the table below and use it to plan your reaction to each piece of advice.

	Advice	Your reaction, e.g. excellent /good/ sensible/ bad, etc.	Your reasons and reactions
Youji			
Fabio			
Stella			

Before you write the diary entry, decide how you will talk to yourself in it.

A. Formally or informally

B. Politely or impolitely

C. Friendly or impersonally

Conclusion to the factual question

How do you make friends in a new school?

Having examined this section, what is your answer to the factual question?

Key and related concepts: Culture and meaning

Before you read Text A

What does the word "culture" mean to you?
Brainstorm your ideas and draw a mind map to represent your findings.

All communities share a range of beliefs, values and interests. People within a community hold shared attitudes, points of view and ways of knowing and behaving. Cultures, just like friendship groups, are dynamic and organic so they can grow and change over time.

When we are learning a language, it gives us opportunities to interact with cultures other than our own. We can learn to interact with others with sensitivity and empathy. One essential aspect of culture is friendship. In this chapter we see that friendships can go beyond our own boundaries and culture. Learning a language allows us to participate in meaningful global interactions, which in turn develops international-mindedness.

What does "meaning" mean?

When we communicate, we send a message to someone. The information contained in the message is the meaning. We find meaning in all forms of communication: speech, writing, visuals, audio and video, as well as any combination of them.

Meaning is complex. We have different **layers of meaning**.

- **Text** is the information in the message.
- **Context** is the situation in which the message is sent.
- **Subtext** is the meaning underneath the surface of the text.

First of all there is **text**. These are the words written down on the page, the images in a picture. These communicate the surface meaning of the text. The four words of the message "BEWARE OF THE DOG" are a warning. We have no further information.

Next, we have the **context**. This is the situation in which the message is communicated. The words, "Beware of the dog" have no context until we create one. If we now add a picture of a dog, we create a **context** for the text.

We now know that the dog referred to in the warning is very big and very dangerous!

Text, context and subtext: A funny story

A postman walks down the street and sees the sign, "BEWARE OF THE DOG". The postman asks himself, "What dog?"

So when the postman says, "What dog?" he sees no danger. But we, the readers, know there is danger. We see that the dog is waiting for the postman. This **context** changes the meaning of the man's question. The **context** gives the message a second meaning.

What is the meaning created by the context?

A. The man cannot read.

B. The dog is hungry.

C. The man does not know what trouble he is in.

Subtext: a deeper meaning

Like a fable or a fairy tale, the story of the man, the sign and the dog can have a moral or a lesson. This subtext is the deeper meaning of the story.

What is the message created by the subtext?

A. You never know what trouble you are in.

B. You must always be careful of dogs.

C. Think before you do something.

Thinking about culture and meaning

In groups discuss the ideas below. It may help you to think about *text*, *context* and *subtext*. Invent a role-play in which a false friend says or does one thing but means something very different.

Text, subtext, context and meaning in visual communication

Criterion 3Ai

Photographs and visuals can have more than one meaning too.

A. How many written texts are there in the picture? *What are the texts?*

B. What is the context? *Why and for what reason did the photographer take the picture?*

C. What is the subtext? *What is the deeper meaning of the picture that the photographer wanted to communicate?*

Formative oral and interactive skills: Layers of meaning

Criterion 3Ciii

Here is a very practical way to think about the concepts of meaning and culture. In small groups, discuss how you tell the difference between true friends and false friends. Ask yourself, "Do friends always say what they mean, or do they say one thing and mean another?" How do you tell the difference between true friends and false friends?

- Do false friends always say what they mean?
- Can they say one thing and mean something else?
- Does a good friend say one thing but do something else?
- How do you know your friends mean what they say?

Denotation is the literal meaning of a word or phrase that might be found in a dictionary.

Connotation refers to the positive or negative subtext that most words or phrases naturally carry with them. So when a true friend says, "I like your hair today" they are really giving a compliment. A false friend may think something very different.

Complete the chart below. Think of the things friends might say to each other (denotation). What does a true friend mean (positive connotation)? What does a false friend really mean (negative connotation)?

> **ATL Social and communication skills**
>
> Work through the section "Layers of meaning" with a partner. Discuss your answers to the questions in this section. Fill in the chart below as a group activity. Here are some useful skills you can develop during this exercise.
>
> - Listening to other perspectives and ideas.
> - Encouraging everyone to contribute.
> - Helping all members of the group to express an opinion.

	Denotation	Postive connotation (True friend)	Negative connotation (False friend)
Ex.	"I like your hair today."	They really want to compliment you.	They are making fun of you. They think that your hairstyle is terrible.
1			
2			
3			
4			
5			
6			

Oral and written text types: Role-play and diaries

What is role-play?

As we have seen, role-play is a speaking activity where you put yourself into somebody else's shoes and you "become" a character for a short time.

While the role-play is taking place the rest of the class can observe and judge the action. Role-plays are useful for acting out imaginary situations. At the end, the other students in your class can assess a character's actions or decisions, and offer feedback.

In this book the situations are based on the texts you read. In role-play you have a chance to practise using English in lifelike situations outside your everyday experiences.

Tips on successful classroom role-play

Role-plays work best when you prepare before you start. Make sure you have prepared the **language** you are going to use. You may want the language on a cue card. Even at more advanced levels you may need time to "get into" the role by thinking about the character you are going to play and the **information** they might have or **opinions** they might hold.

1. Before you start the role-play, with your partner decide what **two** problems this couple has and what the cause of each might be.

Problem 1
A. A relationship problem
B. Money problems
C. A problem at school
D. Other problem

Problem 2
A. A relationship problem
B. Money problems
C. A problem at school
D. Other problem

Planning and scaffolding

Look at the picture below. Working in pairs, imagine you are the two people in the picture.

What is happening? What could be the cause of their argument?

2. Now each person should make notes on the following points to create a cue card for their character. Do not show your cue card to your partner.

Attitude towards the other person
• Helpful or aggressive?
• Friendly or unfriendly?
Feelings towards the other person
• Like or dislike?
Your point of view: problem 1
• Your fault?
• No one's fault?
• The other person's fault?
• Both people's fault?
Your answer to problem 1
Your point of view: problem 2
• Your fault?
• No one's fault?
• The other person's fault?
• Both people's fault?
Your answer to problem 2
Language
A. Formal or informal?
B. Polite or impolite?

ATL Thinking skills

When you are planning your role-play, here are some thinking skills that you can practice:

• Consider ideas from different perspectives.

• Develop contrary or opposing arguments.

• Identify obstacles and challenges.

• Evaluate evidence and arguments.

• Propose and evaluate a variety of solutions.

• Draw reasonable conclusions and generalizations.

3. Once you have each completed your cue card, you can begin your role-play. You should aim to solve both problems.

4. Make sure that the observers have a clear task during the role-play. For instance, they can judge how well, or how badly, the characters behave. Who do they sympathize with? And why?

Formative writing skills: Diary writing

We write diaries to record events, memories, problems, or issues of personal interest.

Typically, a diary entry may contain a mixture of narrative (what happened on that particular day) and comment (to express an opinion about what happened).

Content

A diary entry is a personal account that describes and narrates what you did, saw, or felt on one day. A good diary entry is likely to also contain your comments about these events.

Language and audience

In real life most diaries are private, rather than public. Most diaries are written in the first person: "I did X. I went to Y. I saw Z."

Some diary writers like to write as if they were writing to a best friend. They write to themselves as "you". This is called **direct address**. "Dear diary, you will never guess what happened…"

It is also worth noting the tenses for diaries. If you are writing about events that took place the day before, that is, "yesterday", then you need to write in the **simple past**. "I *came*, I *saw*, I *conquered*." However, you may also write about events that have taken place earlier in the same day, that is, "today". In this case, you may need to use **present perfect tenses** to describe events whose consequences can still be felt. "Today *has been* wonderful. I've finally *discovered* what X is really like."

Tone and style

You can be informal and personal with your use of language – after all, you are writing to yourself! You can also use some slang and emoticons.

You may want to use descriptive language to show your mood and emotions. You can do this through your choice of vocabulary, especially adjectives, adverbs, verbs and nouns.

Structure

In terms of structure, diary entries are often written as narratives – that is, you relate the events in the order in which they took place.

You could also start with a phrase like "What a day this has been!" Or you could start with an opinion: "I have never been so angry before."

You could finish with a final thought. This might be a concluding statement about the events in the diary entry, or a question such as "What will happen next?"

Discussion and debate

Have you ever kept a diary? Do you know people who do?

In groups discuss the reasons why people keep diaries. Are they writing for themselves or for others to read? How can writing a diary help you? Is it interesting to read old diaries?

As you brainstorm ideas, make a visual diagram to help you to record your new ideas.

Formative written activity: Diary writing

Criterion 3Di

Using the advice above, create a diary entry in which you describe an activity or a day out with a friend. Here are some ideas for writing but you could also choose your own topics. Give your work a title.

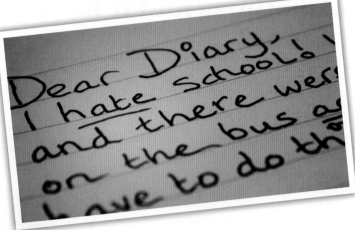

- A day out with your best friend

- First day out with a new friend from a new school

- Meeting a false friend

A note on tenses: if you are writing about an event that took place yesterday, use the simple past (we went) and past continuous tenses (it was raining). If you are writing about an event that took place today, use present perfect tense (we have seen; we have been listening to music).

Planning and scaffolding

Criteria 3Dii, 3Diii

Make notes on the following points to help you to plan what to write.
- Name of friend
- Age
- Background
- I have known X for /since …
- We met when /because … (context)
- Five or more adjectives to describe X
- One thing you don't like about X
- The one thing X always says to you (text)
- What do they really mean? (subtext)
- The one thing X always does (text)
- What do they really mean? (subtext)
- What do you think about the person?

Before you write, think about these issues:
- Will you write in the first person, "I", or the second person, "you"?
- Will you write about your friend using the past or present tenses?
- How will you write to yourself:
  - formally or informally
  - personally or impersonally?

ATL Self-management skills

Try to keep a diary for at least two weeks. Practise your writing by documenting one event and trying to express your thoughts and feelings clearly to yourself. At the end of the two weeks, make a list of all the things you have learned from keeping a diary.

Why can international students sometimes find it hard to make friends?

Conceptual question

Before you read Text C

Discussion points

In your school do you have more friends from your own culture or other cultures?

What are the reasons for this?

In the following exercise you will look at a poster which contains the results of a survey. The survey asked American and international students about their friendships.

While you read Text C

Criterion 3Bi

Reading visual information

Look at the poster, "What makes a friendship?" on the next page. With a partner check that you understand the meaning of the pie charts and diagrams by asking each other questions about the statistics contained in the text.

ATL Research skills

As you work with your partner on this task, you can practise these skills:

- Find, interpret and judge information.

- Collect, record and verify data.

- Access information to be informed and inform others.

- Make connections between various sources of information.

- Create new information.

	Response	Percentage (approximate)
What percentage of international students relate to American students ...	not at all?	
		40%
	about the same as other Americans?	
		20%

	Response	Percentage (approximate)
What percentage of American students relate to international students ...		10%
	less than other American students	
	about the same as other American students?	
		15%

What makes a friendship?

We asked American and international students: How well do you relate to the other group?

INTERNATIONALS

I relate to Americans as well as or better than international students

50%

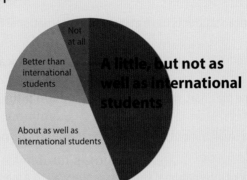

Not at all

Better than international students

A little, but not as well as international students

About as well as international students

AMERICANS

I relate to international students as well as or better than Americans

60%

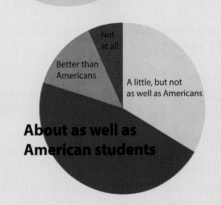

Not at all

Better than Americans

A little, but not as well as Americans

About as well as American students

But when we asked: How many friends do you have from the other group ...

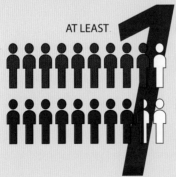

AT LEAST **1**

INTERNATIONALS

AMERICANS

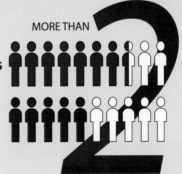

MORE THAN **2**

INTERNATIONALS

AMERICANS

VOA Student Union survey
n=54 American, 56 international

Text C: Text handling

Criterion 3Bi

True/false

Read the table below. The sentences it contains are either true or false. Tick [✔] the correct response.

		True	False
1.	About 80% of Americans have at least one international friend.		
2.	All international students have at least one American friend.		
3.	Half of all American students have at least two international friends.		
4.	Only 20% of international students have at least two American friends.		
5.	According to the pie chart, most Americans relate well to international students.		
6.	Similarly, only a small minority of international students do not relate to American students.		
7.	A large majority of international students relate well to American students.		
8.	The percentage of American and international students that have a lot in common with the other group is about the same.		

ATL Research and communication skills   Criterion 3Biii

1. Look at these findings.
    • Overall, 60% of American students related well to and had friendships with international students.
    • Overall, 50% of international students related well to and had friendships with American students.
    From your own experience, are you surprised by these results? Give reasons.

2. In your school which statement is most usually true?
    A. New students find it easier to make friends with existing students.
    B. Existing students find it easier to make friends with new students.
    C. New students find it easier to make friends with other new students.
    Explain your answer.

Comprehending written and visual text

Study the following table. Rank the techniques used in the poster in terms of effectiveness, with 10 being the most effective and 1 the least. In your opinion, which two techniques are most effective in making the message clear to the reader? Which two are the least effective? Give reasons for your answers.

If you were going to design a poster with similar information about international friendships at your school or in your community, what would you do similarly and what would you do differently? Which techniques would you use in the design of your poster? Complete the table below, giving reasons for your answers.

Techniques	Effectiveness (1 to 10)	Reasons
Different colours		
Visuals		
Statistics		
Different fonts		
Numerals		
Graphs		
Percentages		
Questions and answers		

Techniques	Techniques	Reasons
Different colours		
Visuals		
Statistics		
Different fonts		
Numerals		
Graphs		
Percentages		
Questions and answers		

ATL Thinking skills

Be creative.

When you have made your choices about the techniques you would use, make a sketch of your poster.

- Use brainstorming and visual diagrams to generate new ideas and inquiries.
- Consider multiple alternatives.
- Create novel solutions to authentic problems.
- Make unexpected or unusual connections between objects and/or ideas.
- Make guesses, ask "what if" questions and generate testable hypotheses.
- Apply existing knowledge to generate new ideas, products or processes.
- Create original works and ideas; use existing works and ideas in new ways.

Formative oral and interactive skills: Role-play

Criteria 3Cii, 3Ciii

Your class has been asked to find some activities to welcome new international students to the school. The students are still learning English. You must decide what to do.

ATL Social skills – Collaboration

In this task you can demonstrate that you can work with others effectively and productively.

- Work collaboratively in a team.
- Build consensus.
- Negotiate effectively.
- Make fair and equitable decisions.
- Give and receive meaningful feedback.

Here are some possible activities that the school has suggested.

- Organize a sports day for all students in your year.
- Organize an evening dance for all students in your year.
- Each class organizes a "pot luck" meal where everyone brings a dish.

Do you like these suggestions or can you think of better activities?

Using these suggestions and some of your own, one person should take the role of the teacher suggesting the advantages of these options while the other people should play students who prefer another idea. In the role-play discuss your ideas and come up with a single answer you can agree on.

Planning and scaffolding

Criterion 3Dii

Study this table and use it to help you to think of ideas for the role-play.

	How to organize	How this will help new international students
Sports day		
Dance		
Pot luck class meal		
Alternative suggestion 1		
Alternative suggestion 2		
Alternative suggestion 3		

Formative writing activity: Diary writing – writing about a new student

Criterion 3Di

Your school may receive students from other countries. You may have been one yourself and know what it is like.

A new student has come from abroad. The student is finding it hard to make new friends. You have been asked to look after the student.

Write a short diary entry about the new student. In it you should describe the student and suggest ways the new student can make other friends at your school. You should write between 200 and 250 words. Give your work a title.

Planning and scaffolding
Criteria 3Dii, 3Diii

Before you write

Use this table to organize your ideas for your diary entry. Do not start writing until you have responded to each bullet point.

- Name of new arrival
- Age
- Background
- Think of five or more adjectives to describe the new arrival
- List three things you like about the new person with explanations
- List three things the new arrival might have problems with
- Make three suggestions for making friends at school

Before you write, think about these issues.

- How will you write to yourself:
  - formally or informally
  - personally or impersonally?
- Will you address yourself in the first person, "I", or the second person, "you"?

ATL Self-management skills

In this assignment show that you have the skills to work independently.

- Manage your time and tasks effectively.
- Plan your assignment; meet deadlines.
- Plans your writing.
- Organize complex information.
- Set goals that are challenging and realistic.
- Take action to achieve personal and academic goals.

Conclusion to the conceptual question

Why can international students sometimes find it hard to make friends?

Having examined this section, what is your answer to the question?

What and how does audio-visual Text D communicate about the theme of "Making friends"?

Conceptual question

What do we know so far?

In this chapter you have looked into the topic of making friends. As a class, make a list of the most important ideas you have learned so far in your investigations.

At this stage, are there any points you don't understand?

Make a list of your questions.

How many answers can you find in this audio-visual section?

Suggested texts for this section

A. https://www.youtube.com/watch?v=8ueCG9ZgNFw

How to survive high school: How to make new friends!

B. https://www.youtube.com/watch?v=tPfB6GIjM9Q

International student experience Part 1: Culture shock

C. https://vimeo.com/123526979

Making friends while studying abroad

Note: Alternatively, you could use an audio-visual stimulus of your own choosing related to the theme of making friends.

Before you watch: Text D
Focusing activity
Read through the exercises below to make sure you know what to look and listen for. You may need to watch the materials several times and discuss possible answers in class after each viewing and listening.

While you watch Text D
Criterion 3Ai

Respond to the tasks and answer the questions in the appropriate manner on a separate sheet of paper.

1. This audio-visual stimulus seems to be related to which of these MYP global contexts?
   A. Identities and relationships
   B. Orientation in space and time
   C. Personal and cultural expression
   D. Scientific and technical innovation
   E. Globalization and sustainability
   F. Fairness and development

2. Copy this table and use it to summarize the main points of the stimulus. You may wish to add extra supporting points, if necessary.

	Main idea	Examples and/or explanations and/or details
Subject matter		
Thesis – main point		
Supporting point 1		
Supporting point 2		
Supporting point 3		
Supporting point 4		
Conclusions		

2 **Multiple-choice questions with justifications**

Answer the following questions:

3. The approach to the subject matter of the audio-visual stimulus is mainly:
   A. entertaining
   B. factual
   C. persuasive
   D. other (please specify).
   What is your justification/reason?

4. How would you describe the content of the stimulus?
   A. Very important
   B. Interesting
   C. Fairly interesting
   D. Uninteresting
   What is your justification/reason?

3 **Multiple-choice questions**

Answer the following questions:

5. What was the format of the audio-visual stimulus?
   A. Speech
   B. Conversation/discussion
   C. Debate
   D. Documentary
   E. Other (please specify)   ☐

6. The purpose of the audio-visual stimulus was to:
   A. narrate a story
   B. describe a situation
   C. explain a problem
   D. argue a point of view
   E. give instructions/guidelines
   F. other (please specify).   ☐

7. How many points of view did the audio-visual stimulus show?
   A. One
   B. Two
   C. Three
   D. More than three   ☐

8. The opinions in the audio-visual stimulus are:
   A. very balanced
   B. quite balanced
   C. biased
   D. very one-sided.   ☐

9. How much did the audio-visual stimulus use graphics?
   A. A lot
   B. More than twice
   C. Once or twice
   D. Never   ☐

10. Which of these techniques are used in the audio-visual stimulus?
    A. Voiceover
    B. Special lighting techniques
    C. Music and sound effects
    D. Other special effects
    E. None of the above
    F. All of the above
    G. Some of the above (please specify)   ☐

4 **Formative interactive oral: role-play discussion with the maker of the audio-visual stimulus**

The purpose of this role-play is to find out why and how the video was made.

- One person (the teacher?) volunteers to be the director/ presenter of the audio-visual stimulus.
- One person plays the role of interviewer.
- The rest of class should play the part of an invited studio audience.
- The "interviewer" starts by asking the "director/ presenter" one or two questions and then invites "members of the audience" to ask their own questions.

5 **Formative writing activity: Diary entry**

Write up your reactions to the audio-video stimulus and its contents you have watched in the form of a diary.

Planning and scaffolding

You could mention:
- the reason for watching the audio-visual
- the theme, mains points and conclusion
- the most important conventions and techniques used
- the extent to which the stimulus interested you
- the extent to which you agree with ideas represented in the stimulus.

Use your answers from above to help you plan your diary entry.

The best answers will also give examples and justifications. You should write between 200 and 250 words.

Planning and scaffolding

- Before the role-play, discuss the questions you could ask.
- Use the answers to questions 1–10 on page 30 as the basis for creating questions.

ATL Research and self-management skills

Have you found answers to all the questions you asked at the beginning of this section?

If not, where, and how, do you think you could find the information you are seeking?

Conclusion to the conceptual question

What and how does audio-visual Text D communicate about the theme of "Making friends"?

Having examined this section, what is your answer to the question?

Summative activities

In this summative assessment you will have an opportunity to show your understanding of the topic "Making friends". You will also be assessed on your use of the communication skills you have developed in this chapter. To complete the assessment you will undertake two tasks related to the statement of inquiry for this chapter. Each assessment task requires you to answer a debatable question.

Statement of inquiry

Language is an essential tool that helps us to understand, reflect on and develop close personal, social and cultural friendships in local and global contexts.

Debatable question 1

To what extent should it be the responsibility of teachers and students to make new students welcome?

Debatable question 2

How should you act, and what should you say, to make new friends at a new school?

For the first task you will read two texts and undertake a role-play based on the content. To answer the second question you will watch a video and write a diary entry based on the content.

Summative oral assessment: Role-play

You have had opportunities to practise role-play throughout this unit. In this summative assessment you will have a final chance to show your understanding of the following learning objectives:

B: Comprehending written and visual text

3Bi *Show understanding of information, main ideas and supporting details, and draw conclusions*

3Bii *Understand basic conventions including aspects of format and style, and author's purpose for writing*

3Biii *Engage with the written and visual text by identifying ideas, opinions and attitudes and by making a response to the text based on personal experiences and opinions*

C: Communicating in response to spoken and/or written and/or visual text

3Ci *Respond appropriately to spoken and/or written and/or visual text*

3Cii *Interact in rehearsed and unrehearsed exchanges*

3Ciii *Express ideas and feelings, and communicate information in familiar and some unfamiliar situations*

3Civ *Communicate with a sense of audience and purpose*

D: Using language in spoken and/or written form

3Di *Speak using a range of vocabulary, grammatical structures and conventions; when speaking, use clear pronunciation and intonation*

3Dii *Organize information and ideas and use a range of basic cohesive devices*

3Diii *Use language to suit the context*

Debatable question 1: To what extent should it be the responsibility of teachers and students to make new students welcome?

Assessment task

Read the following texts. Text E gives advice to new students going into middle school. Text F is a blog post by a teacher. He gives advice to other teachers on how to connect with students, especially new ones, and make them feel welcome.

Based on the information you read in Texts E and F below, prepare cue cards and perform a role-play between two or three characters (for instance, a new student, a teacher and another student). The role-play should demonstrate some of the difficulties for new students presented in the texts and show how they can form relationships with other students and teachers.

Consider the debatable question. You should show what you think about the debatable question: To what extent should it be the responsibility of teachers and students to make new students welcome?

The role-play, which could be acted in front of the class or recorded, should allow each person to speak for about 3–4 minutes in total.

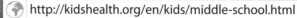
http://kidshealth.org/en/kids/middle-school.html

Moving to middle school

Is it good to be in the middle? Sometimes it's not, like when you're in the middle seat on a long car ride. But sometimes it is, like when you're in the middle of a great movie. What will happen next?

Middle school is a little bit like that. It's called middle school because it's in the middle of your school years. Elementary school is behind you. High school and possibly college still await you.

For a kid, going to middle school often is a big change:

- First, it usually means moving to a new building, which takes some time to adjust to.

- Second, it may mean taking a different bus, with different students.

- Third, friends from elementary school may end up going to different middle schools.

Other things that probably will be different are the teachers and the work. Have you heard rumors that middle school teachers are really mean and the homework is really, really hard? Oh, dear. We've heard those, too, but they're not usually true. Yes, you'll like some teachers better than others, but middle schools are not special breeding grounds for mean teachers!

Learning new stuff

Your homework — and the work you do in class — likely will get more challenging, but that's not necessarily a bad thing. You'll also probably be learning some new and different stuff in middle school — like foreign languages, more advanced courses in computer technology, music and art, health, and life skills.

On top of that, middle school will probably offer a variety of new teams, clubs, and activities you can join. Maybe you love lacrosse, ceramics, or jazz music. You might find opportunities to do all three at middle school.

Visit more than once. Most middle schools have an orientation day for students who will be attending in the fall. Orientation is a day when you tour the school and get a little information about what it will be like to go there.

On the big day, eat breakfast and be brave. You need your energy and brain-power to navigate your new school.

On your way out the door, take everything you need and try to remember that this is a big adventure. You might get lost in the halls. Oh, well, it's your first day! Try to be brave and say "Hi" to other new kids. If you don't know the kid with the locker next to yours, say "Hello." You'll be seeing a lot of each other this year!

In class, listen to what the teacher says and take notes because it's hard to remember everything. Try to write down the important stuff — like your locker combination and your homeroom number. Then you can look it over when you get home and be prepared for Day 2.

Adapted from an article by D'Arcy Lyness, PhD
http://kidshealth.org/en/kids/middle-school.html#

A teacher's blog: Students with the middle school blues

If this is your first year of teaching, I can guarantee one thing: you will never hear middle school students saying they are having the best years of their lives. It's not surprising; it really is an awkward time for them. These kids are going through physical, emotional and social changes. As a result, they are coming under intense pressure. You'll hear it in their voices, you'll see it in their faces.

If you're a new middle school teacher, there are many ways you can help your students. You probably have your own memories and lessons learned from you own middle school experiences.

Here are six pieces of wisdom that I have collected over the years. Feel free to pass them on to your own students.

1. Things get better over time

You have braces that look horrible? You have acne that won't go away? You are in love with someone who doesn't know you exist? These things may seem tragic now, but, in a few years, you'll be able to look back at these troubles and laugh.

2. You don't need to be friends with everyone

Don't try and be too popular. Don't try too hard to be somebody you are not. You don't need to hang out with the most popular kids. Choose your friends carefully. In the next few years you will probably change a lot. Give yourself the space and time to grow. You don't have to please all the people all the time. It's better to make a few good friends now rather than trying to be friends with everyone.

3. Technology makes it easy to ruin relationships.

Technology is great if you use it wisely. These days you can post your thoughts, your feelings, your opinions and your pictures – all in a matter of seconds. But how many times have you put information on the Internet and regretted it two seconds later? It is all too easy to hurt someone, or to damage their reputation. How would you like it if it happened to you? Think first, post later.

4. Dare to be different

Too many middle school kids dress alike, walk alike, talk alike and behave alike.

Stop trying to be like everyone else! Follow your own interests and hobbies; don't stop doing something just because nobody else is doing it. If there's something that really interests you or you have a pastime that fascinates you, follow it and hold on to it. You never know where it will lead.

5. Don't worry too much if you don't yet know where you're going in life

There's plenty of time to find out who you are and where you're going. On the other hand, don't be aimless. Give yourself goals and make sure that you try and reach them to the best of your ability. Use your talents and your gifts, then, when your path becomes clearer, you will find it easier to succeed.

6. Life is full of possibilities

All the changes you are going through are going to lead you somewhere. Who knows what amazing things are just around the corner. Middle school will not last forever. It is just one phase in your life. Remember to have fun, remember to make good choices, remember to hang on to your dreams.

Summative written task: Diary

Debatable question 2: How should you act, and what should you say, to make new friends at a new school?

You have had a few opportunities to practise writing diary entries throughout this unit. In this summative assessment you will have a final chance to show your ability to meet the following learning objectives:

A: Comprehending spoken and visual text

3Ai *Show understanding of information, main ideas and supporting details, and draw conclusions*

3Aii *Interpret conventions*

3Aiii *Engage with the spoken and visual text by identifying ideas, opinions and attitudes and by making a response to the text based on personal experiences and opinions*

C: Communicating in response to spoken and/or written and/or visual text

3Ci *Respond appropriately to spoken and/or written and/or visual text*

3Cii *Interact in rehearsed and unrehearsed exchanges*

3Ciii *Express ideas and feelings, and communicate information in familiar and some unfamiliar situations*

3Civ *Communicate with a sense of audience and purpose*

D: Using language in spoken and/or written form

3Di *Write and/or speak using a range of vocabulary, grammatical structures and conventions; when speaking, use clear pronunciation and intonation*

3Dii *Organize information and ideas and use a range of basic cohesive devices*

3Diii *Use language to suit the context*

Assessment task

Watch the following video about ways of making new friends in new schools (Text G). Write a diary entry describing what you have learned about making friends in new schools. Explain both what to do and what not to do. You may use the information from the texts you have studied in this chapter. The best answers will contain examples and explanations.

The diary entry should be between 200 and 250 words in length.

Text G

How to make friends at a new school (Starting over/moving)

https://www.youtube.com/watch?v=Y4rFCPGLx-0

Going beyond the chapter

In this chapter you have explored how language is an essential tool that helps us to understand, reflect on and develop close personal, social and cultural friendships in local and global contexts. Now make use of the information you have learned and the communication skills you have developed in this chapter for practical purposes beyond the classroom.

Take action! Some suggestions

Role-play

Use the role-play skills you have developed in this chapter to explore the topic of friendship further. You and your classmates in English could share stories or experiences about friendships.

As a starting point you could use these headings:

- making friends at school
- being a new student
- losing friends
- having to change schools
- conflicts with friends.

Dramatize these stories (turn them into short plays/role-plays).

Note: Make sure that real names are changed.

Debate

You can use the role-plays as a way of starting a school-wide debate about friendships.

Here are some topics you might want to act out and then debate.

- How can teachers and students best help new students to feel welcome?

- To what extent should teachers help new students to feel welcome in a new school?

- How should you act, and what should you say, to make new friends at a new school?

- Should schools adapt to new students or should new students adapt to their new school?

- It is better to have one really good friend than to have many acquaintances.

You could make use of any good or interesting ideas or suggestions that have come out of your debate. For example, you could present your findings to the student council or other forum.

Keeping a diary

Try keeping your own diary. Write about events that happen to you each day and your thoughts and feelings.

Service learning

Speak to your MYP coordinator or action and service coordinator to find out your school's expectations for action and service in your particular grade/year.

The ideas below relate directly to the following service learning outcomes:

- discuss, evaluate and plan student-initiated activities
- persevere in action
- work collaboratively with others
- develop international-mindedness through global engagement, multilingualism and intercultural understanding.

Alternatively, you could also use your communication skills to:

- write a guide to being a student at the school from a student perspective
- write a guide for existing students about how to make new students welcome
- create a social event where new students can meet existing students
- create a student blog where students can post ideas for the student council on the topic of friendship
- make students more aware of how people interact with each other. This could be done through a series of role-plays.

Ideas for service

Many schools have a number of new students arriving at the beginning or at some other point during the school year.

Is there a club, group or society at your school that is responsible for welcoming new students and helping them become members of your school community? If not, you might want to start such a club.

If you enjoyed this chapter here are some texts for further reading

Katherine Applegate, *The One and Only Ivan*

Louise Fitzhugh, *Harriet the Spy*

Holly Goldberg Sloan, *Counting by 7s*

Grace Lin, *The Year of the Dog*

Louis Sachar, *Holes*

Jerry Spinelli, *Stargirl*

Sue Townsend, *The Secret Diary of Adrian Mole, Aged 13¾*

Global context: globalization and sustainability

How is everything connected?

In this chapter you will explore the interconnectedness of human-made systems and communities and the impact of decision-making on people and the environment.

The themes of this chapter include the human impact on the environment and our consumption and conservation of natural resources and goods. In this chapter you will explore issues related to recycling both in the home and at school. Later on you will look at different ways schools have developed recycling and other environmentally friendly policies.

Key concept: Communication

Communication is the exchange or transfer of signals, facts, ideas and symbols. As you can see in the picture opposite, communication requires a sender, a message and an intended receiver. Communication involves the activity of conveying information or meaning. In this chapter you will explore how we can use both oral and written interviews to communicate ideas.

Related concept: Structure

Structure is the organization, pattern and elements of text, in any format. Structure helps promote the comprehension and effectiveness of communication. For example, a written structure may involve an introduction, development and conclusion, as in formal essays. However, not all texts use the same structure and you will examine how writers can use different structures to communicate their message.

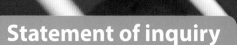

Statement of inquiry

Language plays a very important role in promoting recycling in personal, local and wider communities.

Inquiry questions

→ How much do you recycle at home?

→ What can individuals do to recycle waste?

→ How do you set up a school's recycling programme?

→ What and how does audio-visual text D communicate the theme of recycling?

→ Should a "green school" do more than just recycle?

→ Is recycling the only way for schools to protect the environment?

Before you read Text A

What do you already know about Recycling? Before you begin this chapter, conduct a class brainstorming session. You could start by finding as many ways as possible to finish this sentence, "Recycling means..."

What do you understand by each of the terms in this poster? How are they connected to the idea of recycling? How much recycling do you do:

A. at home
B. at school?

Biodegradable

Compost

Environment

Recycle

Bin

Can

Cardboard

Global warming

Papers

Waste

While you read Text A

On the next page you will find two recycling posters. The first poster gives instructions to homeowners in Swansea, Wales. It explains how to dispose of recyclable household waste, including vegetable matter and garden waste, using the pink and green recycling bags. Other household rubbish that is not recyclable, such as food packaging and broken glass, is collected in black rubbish bags.

The council website says, "There are many, many more things you can recycle, such as clothes, shoes, books, CDs and batteries. We do not currently collect these items from your home but they can be taken to our recycling sites."

The second poster lists 24 household items. On a separate sheet of paper, note which items from the second poster go:

A. in a green bag
B. in a pink bag
C. in a black bag
D. to the recycling site.

Recycling in Swansea

GREEN BAGS

Yes please:

Cardboard

Metal cans

Paper

Glass bottles, jars and foil

No thanks:

Broken glass, plastic of any kind

PINK BAGS

Yes please:

Bubble wrap

Plastic tubs and pots

Plastic bags

Plastic bottles and lids

No thanks:

Foiled wrappers, electrical items, polystyrene, crisp pack, Tetrapaks

wood & timber	hardcore & rubble	paint	scrap metal
food tins & drink cans	mixed glass bottles & jars	garden waste	newspapers & magazines
cardboard	books	batteries	fluorescent tubes
large appliances	small appliances	tvs & monitors	fridges & freezers
plastics	households & garden chemicals	gas bottles	mixed textiles & clothes
used engine oil	car batteries	tyres	discs

Formative oral and interactive skills: Interview questionnaire

Criteria 3Ci, 3Cii, 3Ciii, 3Civ

Work with a partner and ask each other the following questions. Make sure they justify or explain their answers.

Recycling questionnaire

1. On a scale of 1–5, 5 being the easiest, how easy is it to recycle at home?

2. On a scale of 1–5, 5 being easiest, how easy is it to recycle:
   A. cardboard   C. paper
   B. cans   D. bottles?

3. At home you and your family recycle:
   A. always
   B. usually
   C. sometimes
   D. rarely
   E. never.

4. What percentage of your household waste do you think is:
   A. plastic
   B. cardboard
   C. glass
   D. paper
   E. non-recyclable items?

5. In your opinion recycling is:
   A. very important
   B. important
   C. somewhat important
   D. a waste of time.

6. "There are things that I want to recycle but I'm not sure how." Do you agree with this statement?
   A. Strongly agree
   B. Agree
   C. Neutral
   D. Disagree
   E. Strongly disagree

7. Which things would you like to recycle but cannot?

8. If you were given more information about recycling, you would recycle more. Do you agree with this statement?
   A. Strongly agree
   B. Agree
   C. Neither agree or disagree
   D. Disagree
   E. Strongly disagree

ATL Research skills

When you conduct a questionnaire you are practising valuable research techniques.

Which of these skills do you use in the exercise on this page?

- Finding information.
- Interpreting information.
- Collecting and recording data.
- Making connections between various sources of information.
- Creating new information.
- Presenting information in a new format.
- Analysing data to identify solutions and make informed decisions.
- Reporting results.

Planning and scaffolding

As you ask your partner each question write down his or her answers and explanations. You may wish to use this information in a class discussion on your findings at the end of the exercise.

Formative writing activity: Interview

The following exercise is based on the texts in this section. Interview another classmate about his or her recycling habits. Following the question and answer format used above in the recycling questionnaire, copy the chart below and use it to record your partner's answers. Make sure your interview partner gives clear reasons for his or her answers. When you have finished, your partner may interview you.

Write up the interview using between 200 and 250 words for your partner's responses. Write in full sentences.

Planning and scaffolding

Use this chart to record your questions and your partner's responses. You may wish to ask additional questions. You may wish to share and collate the results as a class activity.

Question	Response	Reason/explanation/details
Please introduce yourself.		
1. On a scale of 1–5, 5 being the easiest, how easy is it to recycle at home?		
2. On a scale of 1–5, 5 being easiest, how easy is it to recycle: A. cardboard B. cans C. paper D. bottles?		
3. At home you and your family recycle: A. always B. usually C. sometimes D. rarely E. never.		
4. What percentage of your household waste do you think is: A. plastic B. cardboard C. glass D. paper E. non-recyclable items?		

5. In your opinion how important is recycling?

    A. Very important

    B. Important

    C. Somewhat important

    D. A waste of time

6. There are things that you want to recycle but aren't sure how.

    A. Strongly agree

    B. Agree

    C. Neutral

    D. Disagree

    E. Strongly disagree

7. Which things would you like to recycle but cannot?

8. If you were given more information about recycling, you would recycle more.

    A. Strongly agree

    B. Agree

    C. Neither agree or disagree

    D. Disagree

    E. Strongly disagree

Thank you for talking to me.

Planning and scaffolding Criterion 3Diii

Communicating with a sense of audience

Now think about the language you will use when writing the interview. Choose one of these registers.

- Very formal, as if talking politely to a very important stranger
- Formal, as if talking very politely to people you don't know well
- Informal, as if talking to a friend

Conclusion to the factual question

How much do you recycle at home?

Having examined this section, what is your answer to the question?

Do you think you recycle enough?

Do you recycle too little or too much?

Justify your answers.

45

What can individuals do to recycle waste?

Before you read Text B

Criteria 3Bi, 3Bii, 3Biii

Look at the list of words in the word cloud. How many can you link to the topic of recycling? How are these words linked to the topic?

While you read Text B

Criteria 3Bi, 3Ci

The text below is written in the style of an interview with questions and responses. There are eight sections. Each section has a question and an answer. Here are ten prompts. Match the questions to the answers in the text.

How much can we recycle?	Do we have to throw things out?	What effect does waste have?	Is one person's trash someone else's treasure?	How can we avoid producing waste?
What is nature's answer?	What can we recycle?	What else can we do?	How do we deal with toxic waste?	What questions should we ask ourselves?

http://aries.mq.edu.au/sustainability/

What is waste?

Is this really necessary?

Waste is everything you throw away. It can come from things you buy, from the ways we use water, gas and electricity, and from gas emissions produced by transport.

1 _____ As landfills are filled, we need more space to handle our waste. This is <u>unsustainable</u> because nature is being damaged when we create new landfills and because waste often contains <u>toxic</u> substances.

2 _____ Nature can show us how to <u>reduce</u> the amount of waste we create. We can reuse <u>items</u> before we even start recycling.

3 _____ Can I reuse or repair this? Can I save money by reusing what I already own?

4 _____ If you don't need stuff, give it away for free. Garage sales are a good place to start. You can also take items to a charity store.

5 _____ Almost everything, even batteries and paint cans. Before you buy something, look to see if the product and its <u>packaging</u> are recyclable.

6 _____ Can you <u>purchase</u> an item without all the useless packaging? For example, shop for food at markets where we can buy food without packaging.

7 _____ Turn kitchen waste into high quality soil by composting. Whether you have a big garden or a small apartment, everyone can compost. Your plants will love it!

8 **What else can we do?** Find and use "free stores," clothing exchanges, recycling programmes, and composting centres. Find the closest recycling depots or drop-off centres.

Adapted from http://aries.mq.edu.au/sustainability/ what-to-do/sustainability-at-home.pdf (page 15). Found at http://aries.mq.edu.au/

47

Text handling: Factual assessment of Text B

1 **Finding words with similar meaning**

In the text five words are underlined. Find the word from the right-hand column that could meaningfully replace one of the underlined words from the text on the left. Write your answers on a sheet of paper.

Example: toxic

1. unsustainable
2. reduce
3. items
4. purchase
5. packaging

things
poisonous
possible
sell
buy
cut
parcel
dirty
wrapping
pieces
increase
unworkable

2 **Short-answer questions**

Answer the following questions.

6. What do we recycle by composting?

7. According to the text, why do you think people visit "free stores"?

8. According to the text, what three things can individuals do with waste?

3 **Multiple-choice questions – format and style**

9. What is the purpose of Text B?
   A. To find out opinions about global warming
   B. To find out attitudes to litter
   C. To find out solutions to waste disposal
   D. To find out attitudes to conserving energy resources

10. The structure of the interview is?
    A. A timeline from the beginning to the end
    B. A series of questions and answers
    C. Thesis and supporting points
    D. A definition and examples

11. The language used by the interviewer is?
    A. Very formal and polite
    B. Very casual and personal
    C. Quite casual and personal
    D. Formal and polite

Formative oral and interactive skills: Interview

Work with a partner and record your answers to the following interview questions about household waste. For each answer, give reasons or explanations. You may wish to use information from Text B to help you formulate your answers.

Planning and scaffolding	Criterion 3Civ

Communicating with a sense of audience

Before you begin, think about the language you will use in the interview. Choose one of these registers:

- Very formal, as if talking politely to a very important stranger.
- Formal, as if talking very politely to people you don't know well.
- Informal, as if talking to a friend.

Question	Answer	Reason/Explanation/ Details
Please introduce yourself.		
How important is recycling in today's world?		
What things do you recycle at home?		
What methods of recycling do you use?		
At the moment, what do you do with materials you cannot recycle?		
Would you give stuff away for free or to charity shops?		
Would you be interested in joining a recycling group at school?		
Is there anything else you would like to say on the subject?		
Thank you		

Formative writing activity: Interview

You wish to publish the interview above in the school magazine. Write up your interview notes above using between 200 and 250 words for your answers.

Planning and scaffolding Criterion 3Diii

Organization and language

You could start by introducing the interviewee to your readers.

This introduction could include a little biographical information and your reason for conducting the interview.

Use the question and answer format for the body of the interview.

Will you write up the questions and answers in your interview using:

A. formal language

B. informal language

C. semi-formal language

D. poetic language?

Conclusion to the factual question

What can individuals do to recycle waste?

Having examined this section, what is your answer to the question?

Make a list of all the methods that people could use:

A. at home

B. in school

C. in public.

In class decide which are the most effective methods of recycling available to the general public.

Key and related concepts: Communication and structure

Communication involves the conveying of information or meaning. As we can see in the diagram, communication requires a sender/messenger, a message and an intended receiver/recipient. Study the diagram below. In pairs explain what it is saying about the way in which people communicate messages to each other. Make a list of any points you do not understand.

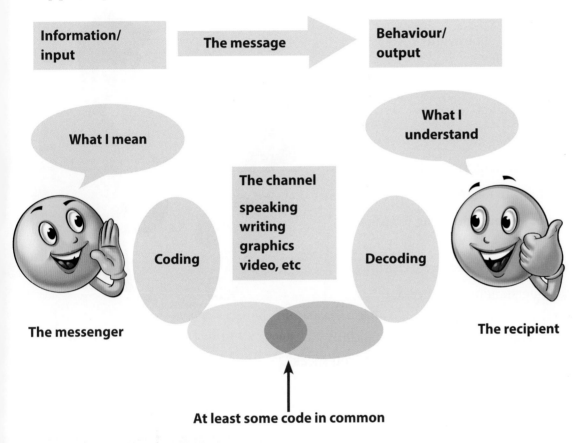

Communication also requires a channel, or medium, for the message, such as speech, writing, graphics or multimedia.

The message is in a code, and the code is language. Different languages use different codes.

As you learn a language, you learn the code. First you learn how to create short, comprehensible messages using simple sentences. As you develop a knowledge of sentence structure, you can communicate your ideas on familiar topics. For example, when first learning a language, you learn how to describe, narrate and give instructions on basic topics such as yourself, your family, food and home.

However, over time you will also want to create more complex texts on more difficult topics, such as conflict resolution, or recycling waste.

In the diagram above, you can see a messenger who creates and sends the message to the recipient, who receives and interprets the message sent.

As messengers, we want to make sure our message is clearly understood. We need to make sure that "What I mean" is the same as "What you understand".

We all know what can happen when the recipient does not understand what we are saying! When we are learning a language, this can become even more difficult. However, when we speak we have many different ways to protect the meaning of our message. We can use facial expressions, a certain tone of voice, hand gestures and body language. When we are speaking to someone, we sometimes repeat words, phrases or ideas.

Sometimes we add little question words such as: "OK?" or "Right?" or "Get it?"

Sometimes we just stop and pause.

Look at the the photograph below.

Imagine their conversation.

Who seems to be doing most of the talking?

What do you think they are talking about?

What methods are the boy and girl using to make sure that:

A. the speaker is sending the message successfully?

B. the recipient is understanding the message correctly?

Think of the way that you use English. What ways do you use to make sure people understand you correctly when you speak?

How do you make sure you are understanding correctly when you are listening to someone?

Do you speak the same way in your first language?

What differences are there in how you speak and listen in your different languages?

ATL Communication skills

Read this passage on learning to communicate in an additional language.

Think about yourself learning English. How many of the ideas in the text can you relate to?

After you have finished reading and reflecting on the text, make a list of points under the heading "Learning to communicate in a new language" and share your ideas with your class.

In order to complete this task successfully, you should:

• review and skim the text again to build understanding

• read critically for comprehension by finding the relevant information from the text

• make inferences and draw conclusions

• take effective notes.

Written structure

When we write, we cannot know for certain how the recipient of our message will react to it. Nor can we do the things we do in speech to make sure our message is understood. We cannot simply repeat or pause or correct ourselves. So one way of making sure that our written message is understood is to have a clear written **structure**. For example, when you write a specific text type such as a short news report, an interview, an essay or a blog entry, you need to organize your writing so that it has a clear beginning, middle and end.

We use different varieties of English depending on whether we are communicating with a close friend or with a stranger such as the manager of a business.

In the same way, we use different written structures depending on what kind of text we are writing.

For instance, would you structure these two texts in the same way or differently?

A. An essay about recycling waste
B. A story about a polluted river

For which text above would you want to write an introduction, well-linked paragraphs using supporting details and/or examples and a conclusion?

How would you structure the other text?

How would you structure a questionnaire about attitudes to littering, waste and recycling? Think about the order in which you would put your questions. Which questions would come first?

Which questions would go in the middle?

Which questions would come last?

Explain your answers to show that you understand the concept of structure.

Discussion and debate

Think about the three written structures we have discussed: the essay, the story and the questionnaire.

In groups think of ways to represent each structure as a diagram that other students could use to plan their writing.

Planning and scaffolding · Criterion 3Diii

Communicating with a sense of audience
Now think about the language you will use in the questionnaire. Choose one of these registers:

* very formal, as if talking politely to a very important stranger
* formal, as if talking very politely to people you don't know well
* informal, as if talking to a friend.

Thinking about communication and structure

Look at the table below. In column 1 you have been given information about the text type, message and messenger. In column 2 choose the recipient of the message.

From column 3 choose the best structure for the text.

Planning and scaffolding

1. Text type, message and messenger	2. Recipient	3. How to structure the text
A blog entry on pollution; **You as yourself**	A. A friend B. A group of people with the same interests C. A stranger D. A community of strangers	A. Beginning, middle and end B. Most important to least important C. Simple to complex D. Main idea, proof and examples, conclusion
A written interview with the manager of a recycling company; **You as journalist**	A. A friend B. A group of people with the same interests C. An important stranger D. A community of strangers E. A teacher	A. Beginning, middle and end B. Most important to least important C. Simple to complex D. Main idea, proof and examples, conclusion
A short story/ fable for children; **You as storyteller**	A. A friend B. A group of people with the same interests C. An important stranger D. A community of strangers E. A teacher	A. Beginning, middle and end B. Most important to least important C. Simple to complex D. Main idea, proof and examples, conclusion
A newspaper article about an accident; **You as journalist**	A. A friend B. A group of people with the same interests C. An important stranger D. A community of strangers E. A teacher	A. Beginning, middle and end B. Most important to least important C. Simple to complex D. Main idea, proof and examples, conclusion
An essay on recycling; **You as student**	A. A friend B. A group of people with the same interests C. An important stranger D. A community of strangers E. A teacher	A. Beginning, middle and end B. Most important to least important C. Simple to complex D. Main idea, proof and examples, conclusion

Formative writing skills: The interview

What is an interview?

One specific text type is an interview. An interview is a structure that allows you to conduct and then write up a person-to-person discussion. An interview can tell us a person's thoughts and feelings on important issues. In an interview, an interviewee talks at length to an interviewer about a specific topic. Some interviews, such as a job or college interview, can be very formal. Some interviews are much more personal.

Look at the picture. What kind of interview is this? What might be the situation?
How will the interviewer and the interviewee speak to one another? What evidence do you have for your responses?

Interview structure

Whatever the situation, a good interview is as carefully structured as a piece of writing. The important structural characteristic is the question and answer format. As a result, before the interview, you need to decide which questions you would like the interviewee to talk about. But you also need to decide in which order to ask your questions.

It makes sense to start with general questions and move to more specific and personal ones.

ATL Self-management skills

Consider the process of learning; choosing and using ATL skills

Think about your writing in other school subjects. Do you use a clear structure when writing?

What different structures do you use?

Make a list of the different ways you can plan a clear structure for your writing.

Which is the better method:

A to think and write at the same time

B to brainstorm for ideas, organize them and then write them down?

For example: in the picture what do you think the two people are talking about? How is the message being communicated? How is the message being received? What is the common code? How do their facial expressions and body language help the messenger and the receiver to interpret the messages?

Introduction

In your introduction, you establish a good rapport with the interviewee. "Thanks for coming in today to talk to XXXX magazine." Or introduce the interviewee. "Ludmila Lewis, you are known as a great supporter of recycling in our school. What is your reason for this?"

The main body

Ask about general issues first and then move to specific questions. For example, begin by asking for some facts. Then you could move on to more difficult questions.

Conclusion or "wrap-up"

Your last question could allow the respondent to provide information about future plans. "So what do you see as the next stage?" You could conclude the interview by thanking the interviewee.

Question types

Closed questions usually begin with a question word such as "When", "Where", "Who". They are usually easy to answer. They can be effectively used at the beginning of an interview to encourage participation and can be very useful in fact-finding. Closed questions usually require short, specific answers.

In an interview use **open questions** such as: "Could you tell our readers about ....?" or "Could you explain/describe/tell ....". An open question starting with "Why" or "How" cannot be answered with a simple "Yes" or "No". Such open-ended questions encourage people to talk, explain their ideas and can produce a large amount of information.

Tone and style

In real life we do not speak the way we write. You need to write your interviewee's responses in complete grammatical sentences but using semi-formal language. You could use some of the ideas in the table below.

	Semi-formal language	Formal language
Vocabulary	**Phrasal verbs** look over come up with	**Formal verbs** analyse develop/invent
Contractions	I'm They **weren't** He **didn't** You**'re**	I am They were not He did not You are
Level of politeness	**Suggestion** I think you are wrong This is not so good. We could...	**Very polite** There may be another way of looking at this. Improvement is possible. I think we may be able to...
Slang	AVOID	AVOID

Use your creative thinking skills to complete this task.

- Apply what you have learned about language and communication in this chapter.

- Make guesses, ask "what if" questions and generate ideas.

Study the picture on the right.

What kind of interview is this? Invent five different scenarios in which the woman is interviewing the man.

What might be the situation?

How will the interviewer and the interviewee speak to one another in each scenario?

Explain each of your responses.

Formative oral and interactive skills: Interview

Criteria 3Ci, 3Cii, 3Ciii

Look at the picture opposite and imagine you are going to interview the student in the photograph about his involvement in recycling. In pairs conduct role-plays in which one person is the interviewer and one person is the interviewee. Reverse roles at the end of the first interview.

Structuring a recycling interview

Think what you will say to introduce the interview.

Write your questions.

Then put the questions into the best possible order (1–10). You may find it helpful to use a table like the one below.

Think how you will conclude the interview.

Opening remarks	
Possible questions	**Structure of interview** *Put your questions in the best order*
A.	1
B.	2
C.	3
D.	4
E.	5
F.	6
G.	7
H.	8
I.	9
J.	10
Wrap up	**Wrap up**

Planning and scaffolding

- In pairs, make a list of about 10 questions to ask the student about his recycling habits and his recycling project.

- **Hint:** You may want to use some or all of the questions from the recycling questionnaire used for Text A.

- Make sure to ask both closed and open questions in the correct order.

Now you can interview your interviewee – the student involved in the recycling project. Decide whether you will use formal, semi-formal or informal language for the interviewer's questions and the interviewee's responses. Make sure you get reasons and explanations for the interviewee's replies.

Criterion 3Civ

Create a table like the one below to record your answers.

Recycling interview notes and structure

Opening remarks		
Question	**Answer**	**Reason/Explanation/Details**
A.		
B.		
C.		
D.		
E.		
F.		
G.		
H.		
I.		
J.		
Wrap up		

Formative writing: Interview

Criteria 3Di, 3Dii, 3Diii

You are writing about recycling for your school magazine. Think about the language you will use in the interview. Choose one of these registers:

- very formal, as if talking politely to a very important stranger

- formal, as if talking very politely to people you don't know well

- informal, as if talking to a friend.

Using the question and answer format, write up your interview with the student above using between 200 and 250 words for your answers.

ATL Social and communication skills

Exchange thoughts, messages and information effectively through interaction; work effectively with others

In this exercise you need to plan carefully with your partner and exchange ideas. As you do so you can develop and demonstrate a number of skills:

- Showing empathy
- Helping others to succeed
- Working collaboratively
- Listening actively to other perspectives and ideas
- Finding areas of agreement and building consensus
- Taking shared responsibility for decision-making
- Giving and receiving constructive feedback

How do you set up a school's recycling programme?

Conceptual question

Before you read Text C

Criteria 3Bi, 3Bii, 3Biii

Focusing discussion

Look at the picture here, then discuss these questions:

- What products are recycled in your school at the moment?
- What is not recycled?
- Could you improve recycling in your school?

How does the picture communicate the idea of recycling?

While you read Text C

Criteria 3Bi, 3Bii

Sequencing the text

In Text C (the table on page 60) there are 10 missing sentences. Copy the table and put sentences 1–10 in the correct order in the text in boxes A–M. Three sentences have been put in place for you.

Text C

Planning a successful school recycling programme

A.	Form a recycling class or club. As a team, define your goals and ensure that each member has a role.
B.	
C.	
D.	
E.	
F.	Contact a disposal company to take away the recycled material.
G.	
H.	
I.	
J.	
K.	
L.	Hold publicity events at your school. Contact the local media.
M.	

1.	Discuss the details of the potential project with teachers, the principal and parents.
2.	Choose one recyclable (for example, cardboard and mixed paper) to start your new programme.
3.	Choose the right type of collection containers. Create clear signs.
4.	Decide where containers should be placed in your school.
5.	Empty the collection bins into your school's larger recycling containers.
6.	Find out what kinds of waste materials there are at your school. Find out which products the school could recycle.
7.	Get approval for the project from the head or principal of your school.
8.	Once your programme is functioning smoothly, expand your programme to include other recyclable materials.
9.	Put trash bins next to the recycling bins or they may be used for garbage.
10.	Share your successes via the school website and magazine.

Would you add any additional or alternative steps to the recycling programme above? Make a new list of steps to include any other points you would add.

Criterion 3Biii

Understanding visual text Criteria 3Bi, 3Bii

First study the poster to the right and in pairs discuss how the paper recycling process works. Here are some communication techniques used to convey ideas in publicity and advertising:

- Colour coding
- Headings
- Repetition and patterns
- Body language
- Structure/composition
- Symbols
- Slogans

Study the poster and list the techniques used to communicate the idea of recycling.

When you have finished the list, evaluate how effective the poster is.

What can you do to improve the poster?

Make a list of points and share them with your class. You may want to create your own poster to demonstrate your suggestions.

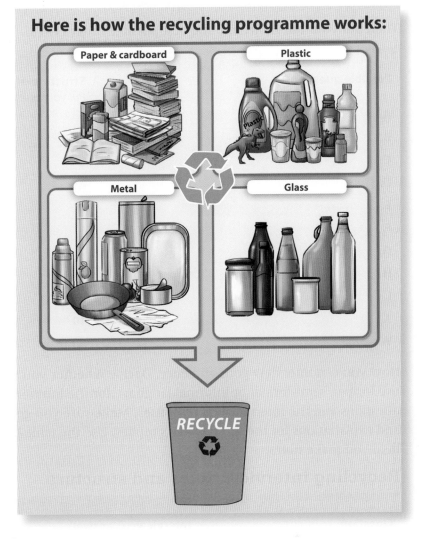

Here is how the recycling programme works:

Paper & cardboard

Plastic

Metal

Glass

RECYCLE

Oral and interactive skills: Interview Criteria 3Ci, 3Cii, 3Ciii, 3Civ

One of the schools in your neighbourhood has decided that they will no longer take part in the district recycling programme for schools. The headteacher says that the programme is too expensive to run and that the children do not benefit from it.

You interview the headteacher of the school.

Decide what open and closed questions you would ask.

Put the questions in a logical order.

Decide on what level of formality to use.

Planning and scaffolding

- One person (possibly the teacher) can volunteer to be the director/presenter of the recycling programme. Criterion 3Dii
- The class should play the part of an invited studio audience.
- The purpose of the role-play is to find out if and how well the recycling programme works.

Structuring a recycling interview

First write your questions.

Then put your questions into the best possible order (1–10).

Opening remarks	
Possible questions	**Structure of interview** *Put your questions A to J in the best order*
A.	1
B.	2
C.	3
D.	4
E.	5
F.	6
G.	7
H.	8
I.	9
J.	10
Wrap up	**Wrap up**

Now you can interview your audience. Decide whether you will use formal, semi-formal or informal language for the interviewer's questions and the interviewee's responses. Make sure you get reasons and explanations for the interviewee's replies. Use the table below to help you make notes.

Recycling interview notes and structure

Opening remarks		
Question	**Interviewee's answer**	**Interviewee's reasons/ explanations/further details**
A.		
B.		
C.		
D.		
E.		
F.		
G.		
H.		
I.		
J.		
Wrap up		

Note: You could record the interview in order to conduct the formative writing activity below.

Formative writing activity: Interview

Criterion 3Di

After interviewing the headteacher who does not want to have a recycling programme at school, you decide to write up the interview for your own personal blog. Your audience is made up of teenagers of your own age.

How do you feel about the matter?

How will you report the interview?

Write up your interview using an introduction to the issue and then use a question and answer format.

Planning and scaffolding
Criteria 3Dii, 3Diii

Put your questions into a logical order.

Write your questions and your interviewee's responses in complete grammatical sentences using semi-formal language. Remember to use the structure and features of a written interview. You are writing about recycling for your own personal blog.

How do you feel about the matter? How will this affect the language you use?

Think about the language you will use in the interview. Choose one of these registers:

• Very formal, as if talking politely to very important strangers.

• Formal, as if talking very politely to people you don't know well.

• Informal, as if talking to good friends.

Write 200–250 words for your answers.

Conclusion to the conceptual question

How do you set up a school's recycling programme?

Having examined this section, what is your answer to the question?

ATL Communication skills

Improving your writing

• Take effective notes.

• Organize your information in a logical manner by using a clear and appropriate structure.

• Write to a specific audience for a specific purpose.

What does audio-visual Text D communicate about recycling?

Before you examine Text D

What do we know so far?

In this chapter you have looked into the topic of recycling. As a class, make a list of the most important ideas you have learned so far in your investigations.

At this stage, are there any points you don't understand?

Make a list of your questions.

How many answers can you find in this audio-visual section?

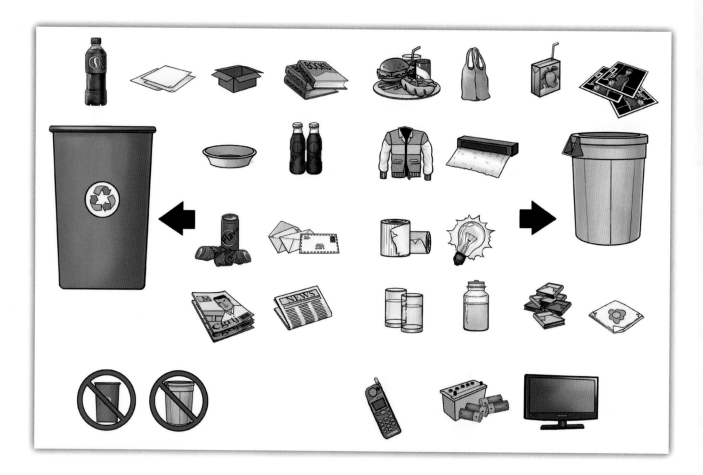

Suggested audio-visual texts for this section

A. https://www.youtube.com/watch?v=oW5W3xjAEaY
Start Your Own School Recycling Program (USA)

B. http://www.abc.net.au/btn/story/s4460241.htm
Recycling in Australia

C. https://www.youtube.com/watch?v=WfwTreAQ1yQ
Recycle Michael initiative launched in schools across Liverpool (UK) to boost the city's recycling rate

D. https://www.youtube.com/watch?v=7LQqgIeT98M
Recycling at your school: You can make a difference

Note: Alternatively, you could use an audio-visual stimulus of your own choosing related to the theme of recycling.

ATL Research skills

Media Literacy

In this section you can develop these valuable 21st Century learning skills.

• Interacting with media to use and create ideas and information

• Making informed choices about personal viewing experiences

• Understanding the impact of media representations

• Seeking a range of perspectives from varied sources

• Communicating information and ideas effectively

Before you watch Text D

Focusing activity

Read through the exercises below to make sure you know what to look and listen for. You may need to watch the materials several times and discuss possible answers in class after each viewing and listening.

While you watch Text D

Understanding the text

Respond to the tasks and answer the questions in the appropriate manner. Write your answers on a separate sheet of paper.

1 1. This audio-visual stimulus seems to be related to which of these MYP global contexts?

    A. Identities and relationships

    B. Orientation in space and time

    C. Personal and cultural expression

    D. Scientific and technical innovation

    E. Globalization and sustainability

    F. Fairness and development

2. Copy this table and use it to summarize the main points of the stimulus. You may wish to add extra supporting points, if necessary.

	Main idea	Examples and/or explanations and/or details
Subject matter		
Thesis – main point		
Supporting point 1		
Supporting point 2		
Supporting point 3		
Supporting point 4		
Conclusions		

2 **Multiple-choice questions with justifications and evidence**

3. The approach to the subject matter of the audio-visual stimulus is mainly:

    A. entertaining

    B. factual

    C. persuasive

    D. other:

Justification/reason:

Evidence from audio-visual text:

4. How would you describe the content of the stimulus?
   A. Really important
   B. Interesting
   C. Fairly interesting
   D. Uninteresting

   Justification/reason:

   Evidence from audio-visual text:

3 Multiple-choice questions – understanding conventions and techniques

Criterion A3ii

5. What was the format of the audio-visual stimulus?
   A. Speech
   B. Conversation/discussion
   C. Debate
   D. Documentary
   E. Other

6. The purpose of the audio-visual stimulus was to:
   A. narrate a story
   B. describe a situation
   C. explain a problem
   D. argue a point of view
   E. give instructions/guidelines
   F. other.

7. How many points of view did the audio-visual stimulus show?
   A. One
   B. Two
   C. Three
   D. More than three

8. The opinions in the audio-visual stimulus are:
   A. very balanced
   B. quite balanced
   C. biased
   D. very one-sided.

9. How much did the audio-visual stimulus use graphics?
   A. A lot
   B. More than twice
   C. Once or twice
   D. Never

10. Which of these techniques are used in the audio-visual stimulus?
    A. Voiceover
    B. Special lighting techniques
    C. Music and sound effects
    D. Other special effects
    E. None of the above
    F. All of the above
    G. Some of the above

Formative interactive oral: Interview with the maker of the audio-visual stimulus

Criterion 3Aiii

Planning and scaffolding

- Before the role-play, discuss the questions you could ask.
- Use the answers to questions 1–10 above as the basis for creating questions.

Note: You will need to record the interview in order to conduct the formative writing activity below. You may wish to copy and adapt this chart and use it to record your questions and answers.

The purpose of this role-play is to find out why and how the video was made.

- One person (possibly the teacher) volunteers to be the director/ presenter of the audio-visual stimulus.

- The rest of class should play the part of an invited studio audience.

- The "audience" interviews the "director/presenter" their questions.

Director interview: notes and structure

Opening remarks		
Question	**Answer**	**Interviewee's reasons/ explanations/further details**
A.		
B.		
C.		
D.		
E.		
F.		
G.		
H.		
I.		
J.		
Wrap up		

Formative writing activity: Interview with the maker of the audio-visual stimulus

Criterion 3Aiii

You are writing about recycling for your school magazine. Using a question and answer format, write up your interview with the director of the audio-visual stimulus using between 200 and 250 words for your answers.

Conclusion to the conceptual question

What does audio-visual Text D communicate about recycling?

Having examined this section, what is your answer to the question?

Summative activities

In this summative assessment you will have an opportunity to show your understanding of the topic of recycling. You will also be assessed on your use of the communication skills you have developed in this chapter. To complete the assessment you will undertake two tasks related to the statement of inquiry for this chapter.

Each task is in the form of an interview. The first outcome is an oral interview with an environmental expert and the second is a write-up of the interview to be published in a youth magazine.

Statement of inquiry

Language plays a very important role in promoting recycling in personal, local and wider communities.

Debatable question 1

Should a "green school" do more than just recycle?

Debatable question 2

Is recycling the only way for schools to protect the environment?

Summative oral interactive task: Interview

Debatable question 1: Should a "green school" do more than just recycle?

Watch Text E and make notes to answer the debatable question.

Use the evidence in the audio-visual text to create an interview between a student reporter and either a member of staff or a student of The Green School in Bali. The purpose of the interview is to find out the answer to the debatable question.

Prepare open questions to allow the interviewee to speak for a minimum of three minutes. Show the questions to the interviewee in advance so that the interviewee can review the video and prepare suitable answers.

The performance of the interview should allow interviewer and interviewee to speak for three to four minutes each. At the end of the interview you may reverse roles to give both speakers a chance to give long answers to the questions.

**Audio-visual text:
"My Green School Dream"**

http://www.ted.com/talks/john_hardy_my_
green_school_dream

Summative oral assessments

You have had opportunities to practise and undertake interviews throughout this unit. In this combined summative assessment you will have a final opportunity to show your understanding of the following learning objectives:

A: Comprehending spoken and visual text

3Ai *Show understanding of information, main ideas and supporting details, and draw conclusions*

3Aii *Understand conventions*

3Aiii *Engage with the spoken and visual text by identifying ideas, opinions and attitudes and by making a response to the text based on personal experiences and opinions*

B: Comprehending written and visual text

3Bi *Show understanding of information, main ideas and supporting details, and draw conclusions*

3Bii *Understand basic conventions including aspects of format and style, and author's purpose for writing*

3Biii *Engage with the written and visual text by identifying ideas, opinions and attitudes and by making a response to the text based on personal experiences and opinions*

C: Communicating in response to spoken and/or written and/or visual text

3Ci *Respond appropriately to spoken and/or written and/or visual text*

3Cii *Interact in rehearsed and unrehearsed exchanges*

3Ciii *Express ideas and feelings, and communicate information in familiar and some unfamiliar situations*

3Civ *Communicate with a sense of audience and purpose*

Summative written task: written interview

Debatable question 2: Is recycling the only way for schools to protect the environment?

Your school has already started a recycling programme. Imagine that you have been asked to write an interview with a teacher from your school. The topic of the interview will be a sustainable project at school that encourages your fellow students to protect the environment.

Read Texts F, G and H and make notes.

Use the evidence in the texts to create an interview between a student reporter and the teacher, in which the teacher gives details of the school's recycling programme. The interview will be published in an environmental magazine targeted at young people. Show the questions to the interviewee in advance so that the interviewee can prepare suitable answers. Record the inteview so that both parties can use the information to write up the interview. Be sure to use the structure and features of a written interview.

Write the text of the interview in between 200 and 250 words.

Summative written assessments

You have had opportunities to practise and write interviews throughout this unit. In this combined summative assessment you will have a final opportunity to show your understanding of the following learning objectives:

B: Comprehending written and visual text

3Bi	*Show understanding of information, main ideas and supporting details, and draw conclusions*
3Bii	*Understand basic conventions including aspects of format and style, and author's purpose for writing*
3Biii	*Engage with the written and visual text by identifying ideas, opinions and attitudes and by making a response to the text based on personal experiences and opinions*

C: Communicating in response to spoken and/or written and/or visual text

3Ci	*Respond appropriately to spoken and/or written and/or visual text*
3Cii	*Interact in rehearsed and unrehearsed exchanges*
3Ciii	*Express ideas and feelings, and communicate information in familiar and some unfamiliar situations*
3Civ	*Communicate with a sense of audience and purpose*

D: Using language in spoken and/or written form

3Di	*Write and/or speak using a range of vocabulary, grammatical structures and conventions; when speaking, use clear pronunciation and intonation*
3Dii	*Organize information and ideas and use a range of basic cohesive devices*
3Diii	*Use language to suit the context*

Energy conservation

School Energy Checklist

Heating and Cooling

- ☐ Set the thermostat 1–2 degrees lower.
- ☐ Find and repair drafts and cold areas of the classroom and school.
- ☐ Install weather stripping, caulking, and insulation as needed to stop air leaks.
- ☐ Keep bookcases and other bulky items away from heating and cooling fixtures.
- ☐ Keep airflows around vents uncluttered and open.
- ☐ Minimize heating and cooling in areas that are not used throughout the day.

Lighting

- ☐ Turn off lights when not in use. Put posters near light switches reminding people to turn off the lights.
- ☐ Reduce use of lights in areas with windows.
- ☐ Use energy-efficient compact fluorescent light bulbs and light-emitting diode bulbs where appropriate.
- ☐ If a room has multiple light switches, turn on only those lights required for the task at hand.
- ☐ Install occupancy sensors to reduce lighting for rooms not in use all day.

Computers, Monitors, and Appliances

- ☐ Turn off computer monitors when not in use.
- ☐ Set controls so that computers will go into sleep mode when not in use.
- ☐ Turn off all computer equipment at the end of the day and on weekends unless your network technicians instruct otherwise.
- ☐ Use Energy Star computers, monitors, printers, copiers, and appliances.

http://www2.gov.bc.ca/assets/gov/education/kindergarten-to-grade-12/teach/teaching-tools/environmental-learning/sustbestpractices.pdf

Text G

Energy-saving ideas for schools

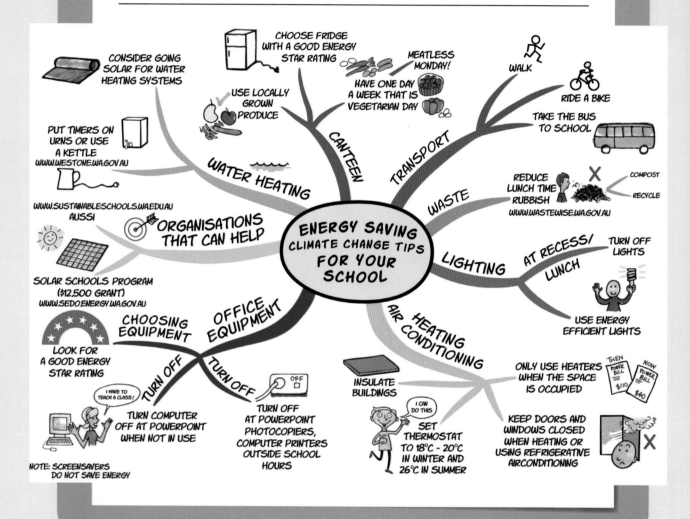

The waste minimization hierarchy

The 3Rs are a simple guide to help each of us minimize waste at work, school and home. Combine the 3Rs with composting and we have a neat package to help us deal with our waste. In minimizing waste, remember to first *reduce*, then *reuse*, and finally *recycle* or *compost* what is left. Remember there will still be some items that will remain rubbish.

Reduce

REDUCE simply means living more carefully so that you have less rubbish to get rid of; avoiding waste is the preferable option of waste management. For example, when shopping look for and purchase products with minimal packaging.

Reuse

REUSE means to use the same item more than once, preferably many times, rather than disposing of it after one use. Reusing saves the energy and resources that would have been used to make a new product and results in less products going into the rubbish bin and ending up in landfill.

Recycle

RECYCLE means to return a waste product to a factory where it is remade into either the same product or something different. For example, many schools recycle paper which is then used to make paper products using a percentage of recycled content. Schools purchasing paper products made from recycled content help to ensure there is a viable market for recycled products. Recycling saves landfill space and also rescues the resources that were used to make the product in the first place. In many cases, recycling can also save energy.

Disposal

When none of the 3R options apply then responsible disposal of the waste is required. The irresponsible disposal of waste includes littering.

Going beyond the chapter

In this chapter you have explored how language plays a very important role in promoting recycling in personal, local and wider communities. Now make use of the information you have learned and the communication skills you have developed in this chapter for very useful and practical purposes beyond the classroom.

Take action! Some suggestions ...

Creating and conducting a survey on recycling

It might be interesting to discover how other students, teachers and parents feel about waste and recycling. You could conduct a survey, which would also show recycling habits of other people in your school and your community. Hopefully, they care more than the young woman on the right.

Make use of the interview skills you have learned in this chapter. Brainstorm a list of open and closed questions that you and your friends might ask others about recycling. Here are some suggestions. You may want to add to the list.

- Do you know the meaning of the term "recycle"?
- Do you recycle? Why?
- Why don't you recycle?
- Do you think you should recycle?
- What materials do you recycle?
- How do you recycle?
- Where do you recycle?
- Do you get paid for recycled materials?
- How much time is devoted to recycling each day or week?
- Do you think you could recycle more?

Put the questions you have selected into a logical order and an easily presentable format.

Interview different groups such as students in other classes, teachers and neighbours. Collate the results, noticing similarities and differences in the responses.

Present your findings to your class or publish your results in a school publication.

Service learning

Speak to your MYP coordinator or action and service coordinator to find out your school's expectations for action and service in your particular grade/year.

The ideas below relate directly to the following service learning outcomes:

- become more aware of their own strengths and areas for growth
- undertake challenges that develop new skills
- discuss, evaluate and plan student-initiated activities
- persevere in action
- work collaboratively with others
- develop international-mindedness through global engagement, multilingualism and intercultural understanding
- consider the ethical implications of their actions.

Ideas for service

Using the action idea above, review how paper and other products are being overused at your school and propose ideas on how to reduce excess waste and promote recycling or re-usage.

Use resources such as TED, TEDx or Edutopia.org to research what other schools are already doing in terms of environmental projects. Use this research to help plan your community project or other service-learning project.

Conduct research on how certain waste products such as paper and glass are recycled at your school. Find out what happens to the recycled materials.

If you enjoyed this chapter here are some texts for further reading

- The Earthworks Group and Sophia Javna, *The New 50 Simple Things Kids Can Do to Save the World*
- Linda Booth Sweeney, *Connected Wisdom: Living Stories About Living Systems*
- Jenn Savedge, The Green Teen, *The Eco-Friendly Teen's Guide to Saving the Planet*
- Carl Hiaasen, *Hoot*
- Gail Gauthier, *Saving the Planet & Stuff*

ATL Research and thinking skills

At the end of any learning experience always ask yourself these questions:

- What lessons have I learned from this chapter?
- What concepts don't I yet understand about this topic?
- What questions do I still have about this topic?
- Where can I find answers to these questions?

3 Resolving conflict

Global context: Fairness and development

What are the consequences of our common humanity?

In this chapter we will explore the themes of sharing finite resources, conflict and its resolution. We will look at a series of teaching stories from around the world to see what each story can teach about how and why arguments can lead to conflict and then how those conflicts can be peaceably resolved.

Key concept: Connections

Connections are links, bonds and relationships among people, objects, organisms or ideas. Connections exist across time and across cultures. This concept is central to the study of language and allows for the exploration of the relationships between text, creator and audience. We shall also explore how language can both disrupt and heal the connections between people.

Related concept: Empathy

Empathy is an attitude of understanding, an emotional identification with a person, character, argument or situation. We will examine how empathy is an essential tool in creating relationships and in the process of conflict resolution.

Statement of inquiry

Stories are almost always about conflict. They connect cultures by describing the universal ways and means of resolving personal and global differences.

Inquiry questions

→ What are facts, and what are opinions?

→ What skills do we need to resolve our differences?

→ What happens when we use force to solve our problems?

→ What and how does audio-visual text D communicate about the themes of conflict and resolution?

→ Is conflict avoidable?

→ Can a story teach us how to solve a conflict?

1919-114

What are facts, and what are opinions?

Before you read Text A

Criteria 3Bi, 3Biii

What do you know about theme of conflict resolution? Before you begin this chapter, conduct a class brainstorming session. You could start by asking, "In real life, how do people solve their differences?"

An important part of learning a language is determining what a fact is and what an opinion is.

A **fact** is a statement that is true and can be proven objectively. A fact must have evidence and examples to prove that it is correct.

For example, "London is the capital city of the UK" is a fact.

An **opinion**, however, is a statement that is a belief; it states what someone feels or believes to be true.

For example, "London is the greatest city on Earth" is an opinion.

1. List another ten facts about London.

2. List ten more opinions about London or another city of your choice.

Before you read Text A

Conflict can occur when one or both sides insist on arguing their respective points of view as if their opinions were facts.

Consider the picture below which portrays a folk tale set in Thailand. There are six blind men and an elephant. They have never met an elephant before and want to learn about the animal.

How to tell the difference between a fact and an opinion

- What facts can they learn by touching the elephant?

- What other senses can they use to learn about the elephant?

- What problems might the six blind men have when describing the elephant?

Text A: Part 1

Six blind men and an elephant

Long ago six old men lived in a village in India. Each was born blind. Since the blind men could not see the world for themselves, they had to imagine its wonders. They listened to the stories told by travellers to learn what they could about life outside the village.

They were most curious about elephants. They were told that elephants could knock down trees, carry huge weights, and frighten people with their loud trumpet calls. But they also knew that the king's daughter rode an elephant when she traveled in her father's kingdom. Would the rajah let his daughter get near such a dangerous creature?

The old men argued day and night about elephants. "An elephant must be a powerful giant," said the first blind man. He had heard stories about elephants being used to clear forests and build roads.

"No, you must be wrong," argued the second blind man. "An elephant must be graceful and gentle if a princess is to ride on its back."

"You're wrong! I have heard that an elephant can pierce a man's heart with its terrible horn," said the third blind man.

"Please," said the fourth blind man. "You are all mistaken. An elephant is nothing more than a large sort of cow. You know how people exaggerate."

"I am sure that an elephant is something magical," said the fifth blind man. "That would explain why the rajah's daughter can travel safely throughout the kingdom."

"Elephants don't exist at all," declared the sixth blind man. "No such animal can do all these things."

While you read Text A

Criterion 3Bi

Analysis of Part 1

In this section of the story, each of the six blind men has a different opinion about what an elephant is like. Copy the table below and answer the questions by filling it in.

	This man thought the elephant …	What reason did each blind man give for his opinion?
The first		It can clear forests and build roads.
The second		
The third	was dangerous	
The fourth		
The fifth		
The sixth	did not exist	

While you read

Analysis of Part 2

The six blind men each feel a different part of the elephant. Copy the chart below and answer the questions by filling it in.

	What part did he touch?	What opinion did he come to?	What were his reasons?
The first		The elephant is like a …	It is smooth and solid
The second			The tail and the snake are similar.
The third			
The fourth			
The fifth			
The sixth			

Text A: Part 2

Finally, the villagers grew tired of all the arguments, and they arranged for the curious blind men to visit the palace of the rajah to learn the truth about elephants. A young boy from their village was selected to guide the blind men on their journey. The smallest man put his hand on the boy's shoulder. The second blind man put his hand on his friend's shoulder, and so on until all six men were ready to walk safely behind the boy who would lead them to the rajah's magnificent palace.

When the blind men reached the palace, a gardener from their village who worked in the palace grounds greeted them. Their friend led them to the courtyard. There stood an elephant. The blind men stepped forward to touch the creature that was the subject of so many arguments.

The first blind man reached out and touched the side of the huge animal. "An elephant is smooth and solid like a wall!" he declared. "It must be very powerful."

The second blind man put his hand on the elephant's trunk. "An elephant is very deadly. It is like a giant snake," he announced.

The third blind man felt the elephant's pointed tusks. "I was right," he decided. "This creature is as sharp as a spear."

The fourth blind man touched the elephant's legs. "See! It has four legs. What we have here," he said, "is an extremely large cow."

The fifth blind man felt the elephant's giant ear. "I believe an elephant is like a magic carpet. It that can fly over mountains and treetops," he said.

The sixth blind man gave a tug on the elephant's coarse and dry tail. "Why, this is nothing more than a piece of old rope."

Text A: Part 2

The gardener led his friends to the shade of a tree. "Sit here and rest for the long journey home," he said. "I will bring you some water to drink."

While they waited, the six blind men talked about the elephant.

"An elephant is like a wall," said the first blind man. "Surely we can finally agree on that."

"A wall? An elephant is a giant snake!" answered the second blind man.

"It's a spear, I tell you," insisted the third blind man.

"I'm certain it's a giant cow," said the fourth blind man.

"Magic carpet. There's no doubt," said the fifth blind man.

"Don't you see?" pleaded the sixth blind man. "Someone used a rope to trick us."

Their argument continued and their shouts grew louder and louder.

"Wall!" "Snake!" "Spear!" "Cow!" "Carpet!" "Rope!"

"Stop shouting!" called a very angry voice.

Text A: Part 3

It was the rajah, awakened from his sleep by the noisy argument.

"How can each of you be so certain you are right?" asked the ruler.

The six blind men considered the question. And then, knowing the rajah to be a very wise man, they decided to say nothing at all.

"The elephant is a very large animal," said the rajah kindly. "Each man touched only one part. Perhaps if you put the parts together, you will see the truth. Now, let me finish my nap in peace."

When their friend returned to the garden with the cool water, the six men rested quietly in the shade, thinking about the rajah's advice.

"He is right," said the first blind man. "To learn the truth, we must put all the parts together. Let's discuss this on the journey home."

The first blind man put his hand on the shoulder of the young boy who would guide them home. The second blind man put a hand on his friend's shoulder, and so on until all six men were ready to travel together.

After you read Text A

Analysis of Part 3
Short-answer questions

1. According to the rajah, why were the men quarrelling?

2. What lesson did the blind men learn about truth?

3. What lessons does the story teach us about trusting our senses?

4. By reading the story, what lessons do we learn about facts and opinions?

Discussion and debate

The story of the six blind men and the elephant asks us to think about whether we can trust our senses. What do you think? In what ways are our senses useful for understanding the world around us? Are there times when we should not believe what our senses tell us?

Study the picture. How many legs does the elephant have?

What is happening?

Optical illusions create images that can trick our brains into seeing things that are not

Another elephant – How many legs?

"real". The eye gathers information and the brain processes that information. The brain interprets what it sees and tries to make sense of it. But, in the case of an illusion, the brain perceives an image that does not match the "true" image. So an optical illusion simply tricks our brains into seeing things which may or may not be real.

Look up more of these illusions on the Internet and discover for yourself just how tricky it can be when your brain cannot accurately interpret the images you are seeing.

ATL Thinking and social skills

This section of the chapter asks us to separate facts from opinions.

What do we learn from the story of *The Six Blind Men and the Elephant?*

What is an opinion?

What is a fact?

Why is it important to distinguish facts from opinions when settling an argument?

Which of the following techniques does the Rajah use to settle the argument between the six men?

- Listens actively to other perspectives and ideas.
- Shows empathy towards others.
- Encourages the others to give their opinions.
- Gives others the responsibility for decision-making.
- Helps others to understand.
- Demands to have his own way.
- Takes responsibility for his decisions.
- Manages and resolves conflict by working collaboratively.
- Builds agreement.
- Makes fair and equitable decisions.
- Negotiates with others.
- Shows leadership.
- Gives meaningful advice.

Formative writing activity: Reasoned argument

In the story, the rajah gives a "reasoned argument" in a series of statements to the six blind men. He uses evidence and reasoning to persuade them that they are all wrong.

For example, he says, "The elephant is a very large animal. Each man touched only one part. Perhaps if you put the parts together, you will see the truth."

Retell the story from the moment the rajah wakes up. Start here: '"Stop shouting!" called a very angry voice. It was the Rajah.'

In your version, the rajah explains to each of the blind men why he is wrong. Write between 200 and 250 words.

Now copy the table below and complete the rajah's words to the six blind men.

Discussion and debate

A reasoned argument uses which way of knowing?

A Sense perception

B Strong emotions

C Logic

You want to convince someone that your ideas are correct. In what ways are reasoned arguments better than emotional ones?

Planning and scaffolding — Criterion 3Dii

As part of your story, the rajah speaks to each man, using a reasoned argument.

For example, the rajah might have said to the first blind man: "You say the elephant is a wall. This is because you felt something smooth and solid. But not everything that is smooth and solid is a wall."

The rajah said to	You say the elephant is like …	This is because …	However, this is not correct because …
the first blind man			
the second blind man			
the third blind man			
the fourth blind man			
the fifth blind man			
the sixth blind man			

Planning and scaffolding — Criterion 3Dii

Communicating with a sense of audience

Now think about the language you will use in the story. Choose one of these registers:

- very formal, as if writing to a very important stranger
- formal, as if writing very politely to an audience you don't know well
- informal, as if talking to a friend.

Formative oral activity

Criteria 3Ci, 3Cii

Now that you have completed the reasoned argument, use your written text to create a speech. In this instance use the chart above to give the rajah's speech to the six blind men.

As part of your assessment for English Language Acquisition, you will undertake a series of interactive oral tasks that will last for three or four minutes per person. Some of these activities you will do as a part of a group or in pairs, but sometimes you may need to speak on your own. One such instance is when you make a speech.

Making a speech in public can be quite a difficult experience, so it is important to practise. In this chapter you will learn a variety of techniques to help you to make speeches. However, in this instance, you can practise by simply recording yourself and listening and watching the playback.

As you watch the recording make two lists:

- things I do well
- things I can do better.

Conclusion to the factual question

What are facts, and what are opinions?

Having examined this section, what is your answer to the question?

Planning and scaffolding

Address your audience   Criteria 3Ciii, 3Civ

How will the rajah speak to the six blind men?

A. Formally

B. Semi-formally

C. Informally

Give your reason.

Make sure the audience understands the purpose of the speech

Why is the rajah talking to the six blind men?

Give evidence, examples and explanations for each key point.

Use the information you added in the chart above on page 84 to speak to each of the six blind men.

Have a strong conclusion

What is the rajah's conclusion?

Explain what you want to happen

According to the rajah what should the six blind men do in future?

Formative oral and interactive skills – Speeches

Oral interactive skills: Speech

Criterion Biii

As we said above, public speaking in any language can be very stressful, even more so if you are still learning the language. Below are some guidelines to help you.

Step 1: Structure your ideas

- Structure your talk with a clear beginning, middle and end.

- Start your talk with a powerful, attention-grabbing introduction.

- Explain what you are going to talk about. Tell them your topic and your thesis or "big idea".

- Make a series of clear points to support the thesis.

- Come to a clear conclusion.

Step 2: Use signposting language to help the audience to understand your talk

Greet your audience	Good morning/afternoon
Introduce your carefully defined topic	I'd like to talk to you about …
Explain the topic area and purpose	I am going to show that …
Or briefly preview the organization of the body of your talk	The main points I will make are firstly …, secondly … and thirdly … .

Give examples to make your points clear. Use expressions such as:

"For instance …"

"Take … for example …""

"To give you an example …"

"A case in point is …"

"To illustrate this …"

"To show you what I mean …"

Step 3: Practise what you are going to say

ATL Self-management and communication skills

After reading this section on speeches, review, revise and improve "The rajah's speech" that you gave in the previous section.

This exercise will give you an opportunity to develop strategies for improving your production skills.

Ask yourself, "What can I already do?", "What don't I yet understand?", "What shall I work on next?"

- Consider your existing content.

- Identify your strengths and weaknesses.

- Develop new techniques and strategies for effective learning.

Conflict resolution – a case study

Tamara's mother makes her baby-sit for her brothers whenever she is busy or has to work. This happens three or four times a week.

Tamara's teacher has been complaining because Tamara doesn't get her homework done. The teacher thinks Tamara is not working. But Tamara says she does not have any quiet time to do her homework because her brothers need attention all the time.

You are going to give a speech about the problem outlined above. The purpose of the speech will be to identify the causes of a conflict and offer a solution that works for everybody.

ATL Thinking skills

How does this problem show the difference between facts and opinions?

Analyse and evaluate issues and ideas

• Recognize unstated assumptions and bias.

• Evaluate evidence and arguments.

• Recognize and evaluate propositions.

• Test generalizations and conclusions.

Discussion and debate

1. What are the opinions of:
   A. the mother
   B. the teacher
2. According to Tamara, what are the facts in the situation?

Speech: Scenario

You are the school counsellor. Tamara comes to you to discuss her problems with her mother and her teacher. You listen carefully and can empathize with her situation. As a counselllor, you think her mother is not being reasonable and you also think that the teacher does not understand the situation properly. You agree to speak to Tamara's mother and the teacher at a meeting. You will explain the problem to both of them from Tamara's point of view.

What will you say?

How will you organize what you say?

Planning and scaffolding	Criteria 3Ci, 3Cii, 3Ciii, 3Civ

Use the outline below to help you organize your main ideas.

1 Explain Tamara's problem here:		
2 Write the points of view of the mother and the teacher below.	The counsellor's response to the person's argument	The counsellor's reasons and explanations
The mother's point of view is …		
The teacher's point of view is …		
3 The counsellor's conclusions		
What does the mother need to do?		
What does the teacher need to do?		

Conclude by saying how this advice will help Tamara:

How can you use signposting language such as connectives to help your audience understand your ideas?

You should practise and rehearse your speech to make sure that you are confident when you give your speech in class.

Formative writing: skills

Explanation

Reasoning is a logical, thoughtful way of thinking. It allows you to hold an opinion and back it up with facts. In language it is a really important and useful skill to learn. For example, in language acquisition there are many situations when you need to persuade someone to do something, or to agree with your opinion on a matter.

One way you can achieve your goal is by making a **reasoned argument.** As we have already seen in this chapter, a **reasoned argument** consists of one or more statements (reasons) that provide support for a point of view. For example, when your school directors explain the reasoning behind new classroom rules, they make it clear exactly why and how they introduced them.

Planning and scaffolding
Criterion 3Civ

Communicating with a sense of purpose

Now think about the language the characters will use in the speech. Choose one of these registers:

- Very formal, as if talking politely to a very important stranger.
- Formal, as if talking very politely to people you don't know well.
- Informal, as if talking to a friend.

Structure

Here are three different structures for your argument:

- **The "one-sided" approach:** Support a single point of view, either for or against. Justify each point you make by giving an example and/or an explanation. Write a strong conclusion about what should be done.

- **The "balanced but undecided" approach:** There is no single right answer to a problem. State that both sides have valid arguments. Or say that both sides have weak arguments. Give reasons for supporting or criticizing both sides. Conclude by saying that the different sides should recognize that they both have valid points and they need further discussion.

- **The "emotion versus logic" approach:** You have one argument based on logic but there is another one based on what your heart tells you. State both and support both arguments with examples. Which argument is better? Which idea is more clearly stated? Conclude, stating which side you would support and why.

The heart (emotion) defeats the brain (logic).

Reasoned argument: scenario

Jack tells you he cheated in the maths test yesterday. He copied some answers from Lucy, who was sitting next to him. He tells you that his parents are putting pressure on him because he is not doing very well in maths. He also says he is not the only person cheating and it was just a matter of few marks.

- What should you say to Jack?

- What action should you take?

- Can you empathize with his situation?

- But do you agree with his actions?

Formative writing activity: Reasoned argument

Criteria 3Di, 3Dii, 3Diii

You decide to send Jack an email. Copy and use the chart below to write out a reasoned argument based on the scenario above about what you would say and do if you knew that Jack had cheated in his maths test. Write between 200 and 250 words.

The problem		
Your approach	One-sided/balanced/emotion versus logic?	
Jack's arguments	Your response	Reason and explanation
Parents' pressure		
Everyone is doing it		
It was only a few answers		
Your conclusion	What will you do about the situation?	

What skills do we need to resolve our differences?

Before you read Text B

Criterion 3Bi

Focusing discussion

Here is a list of different ways people solve problems and disagreements.

Appreciating differences

Brainstorming

Bullying

Cooperating with others

Damaging property

Dominating others

Empathizing

Exchanging ideas

Excluding people

Getting someone else's opinion

Hitting something

Including people

Insulting

Keeping quiet/not contributing

Listening carefully

Mediating

Name-calling

Punishing

Respecting other people's ideas

Refusing to take part

Seeing things differently

Sharing ideas

Shouting

Speaking before thinking

Swearing

Taking part in activities

Talking about problems

Thinking before speaking

Violence

Can you add other methods of problem-solving to each list: useful for solving conflicts; not useful for solving conflicts?

ATL Social skills

Look at the list opposite and the ideas you have added.

Choose the top five strategies that will help you when you are working in class in pairs or small groups?

Choose the five actions which are the most negative and unhelpful when working in groups?

While you read Text B1 and B2

Criterion 3Bi

Two stories of conflict and resolution

Stories connect cultures by describing common conflicts. They also teach us the ways and means of resolving our personal differences. Here are two stories that teach conflict resolution.

Each story tells of an argument. Read each one and identify:

- the people involved in the conflict

- the matter they are arguing about

- the ways the people try to resolve their arguments

- the methods used to resolve the argument or the problem.

You will also try to identify the real problems underneath the argument. See the previous page for a list of good and bad methods of conflict resolution.

ATL Thinking skills

In this section you will use a number of critical thinking skills:

- Analyse and evaluate issues and ideas.

- Recognize unstated assumptions and bias.

- Evaluate evidence and arguments.

- Recognize and evaluate propositions.

- Test generalizations and conclusions.

Text B1

The two sisters who fought over an orange

Once upon a time there were two sisters. They were always arguing. They lived in the same street and one day they both noticed an orange that had fallen off the back of a cart. Oranges were rare in those days, and so the two women both ran for the orange and reached out for it at the same moment. Together their hands grabbed the orange and neither would let go.

They argued for hours over who should have the orange. The older sister said she had seen it first. The younger said that the orange had fallen onto the side of the street where she lived. Neither would give way, so together they took the orange to their mother. She heard their stories carefully and then said that she would cut the orange in half. Each sister should have one half of the orange. Satisfied, the two women went home.

When she reached home, the first sister peeled her half of the orange, ate it and threw away the peel. Across the road, her sister peeled her half of the orange, threw away the fruit inside, and used the peel to make marmalade.

After reading Text B1

Criterion 3Biii

Now that you have read the story of the The Two sisters and the Orange, identify:

• the people involved in the conflict

• the matter they are arguing about.

Look again at the list of ways of resolving conflict on page 91. Identify the methods used by the mother to resolve the argument. Do you think the mother and the two sisters find the best possible solution to their quarrel?

What advice would you have given the two sisters in the same situation?

In your opinion what are the real reasons that the sisters are fighting over the orange?

Text B2

Seventeen camels, three brothers and a wise man

A father's will stated that his eldest son should get half of 17 camels while the middle son should be given one-third. The youngest son should be given one-ninth of the 17 camels.

As it is not possible to divide 17 into half or 17 by 3 or 17 by 9, the three sons started to fight with each other.

A pause for thought

• Do you have any thoughts about how to divide 17 camels among three sons as prescribed in their father's will?

• Is it possible to divide the inheritance without killing at least one camel?

Brainstorm the problem in class. What solutions can you find?

So, the three sons decided to go to a wise man. The wise man listened patiently as they told him about the whole matter. After giving thought to the problem, the wise man brought one camel of his own and added it to the 17 camels from the father. That increased the total to 18 camels.

Now, the wise man started reading the father's will.

One half of 18 is 9. So he gave the eldest son 9 camels

One third of 18 is 6. So he gave the middle son 6 camels

One ninth of 18 is 2. So he gave the youngest son 2 camels.

Now add this up: 9 plus 6 plus 2 is 17 and this leaves one camel, which the wise man took away.

After you read Text B2

Criterion 3Biii

In your opinion what are the real reasons for the conflict about the camels? Look again at the list of ways of resolving conflict on page 91. Identify the methods used by the wise man to resolve the argument.

Here are eight creative thinking techniques. Which of these does the wise man use?

Generating novel ideas and considering new perspectives

1. Consider multiple alternative solutions, including what might seem impossible.

2. Create imaginative ideas.

3. Create new solutions to real problems.

4. Design improvements to existing technologies.

5. Generate metaphors and images.

6. Make guesses, ask "what if" questions.

7. Make unexpected or unusual connections between objects and ideas.

8. Use brainstorming to generate new ideas and inquiries.

Discussion and debate

Now that you have read both stories in this section, decide which conflict has a better resolution.

After you have made your choice, give a set of reasons why the one solution is better than the other.

Role-play – conflict resolution

Look at the picture on the right.

What do you think is happening?

What could the argument be about?

How are such fights and arguments resolved in your school?

You might want to discuss the issue with your teacher.

Now read on.

Poppy and Leila are good friends, but they both like Hector.

Their classmate, Nina, tells Poppy that Leila has been saying nasty things about her, Poppy, to Hector. Poppy believes what Nina tells her and confronts Leila after school. They have a huge argument.

The next day Leila has a second argument. This time it is with Nina. Poppy watches. Hector tries to stop the fight. The teacher on duty sees what is happening and calls all four students to come to a meeting.

Planning and scaffolding

In groups now conduct a role-play in which the teacher talks to each of the three girls, and Hector to find out what has happened.

In the role-play, the teacher needs to find answers to the questions below.

- Who is involved in the matter?
- How many different problems are there?
- Identify the different problems
- For what reasons is each student involved in the fight?

  Poppy:

  Leila:

  Nina:

Discussion and debate

Imagine you are the teacher. What would you do to understand and resolve the arguments between the four students?

Study the diagram opposite: How to analyse a conflict. Use it to find solutions to the conflict.

What advice would you give to each person in order to avoid more conflict?

- To Poppy?
- To Leila?
- To Nina?
- To Hector?

How to analyse a conflict

Reasons and causes

Solutions to conflict

Conflict

Effects of conflict

Different people involved

Conclusions

Look again at the list of conflict resolution strategies on page 91. Which strategies does the teacher use to solve the arguments between the students?

95

Formative oral and interactive skills: Speech

When you undertake to give a speech, you have to speak for 3 or 4 minutes. In this practice exercise, imagine you are the teacher. After the argument, you need to talk to Hector, Nina, Leila and Poppy together. What would you say to each one in turn?

Planning and scaffolding

Before you speak to the students, make sure you know exactly what you want to say. In groups prepare for the speech by completing the chart. Use it as a cue card to deliver your conflict resolution speech to the students.

Reasons for talking to the students	Conflicts: Effects on the school:		
	What he/she has done	Why this creates a problem for someone else	What the person could do to make the situation better
Leila			
Poppy			
Nina			
Hector			
Conclusions: What resolution are you looking for?			

Planning and scaffolding

Communicating with a sense of audience

Now think about the language the teacher and the four students will use in the conversation.

How will the teacher talk to the students?

How will the students talk to the teacher?

How will the students talk among themselves?

What register will you use in each instance:

A. formal or informal

B. polite or impolite

C. friendly or impersonal?

You will need to practise your speech individually. Rehearse by recording yourself. Remember to:

- set realistic goals
- take action to achieve your goals
- use appropriate strategies for organizing complex information
- practise, practise, practise.

Formative writing skills: Criteria 3Di, 3Dii, 3Diii
Reasoned argument

As a result of the incident above, the teacher needs to write an incident report for the head of school. Using a reasoned argument, explain what has happened and how you have dealt with the matter. Use formal language. The table you completed on the previous page can help you with this.

Conclusion to the conceptual question

What skills do we need to resolve our differences?

Having examined this section, what is your answer to the question? What are the best and worst ways of resolving a conflict?

Key and related concepts
Connections and empathy

Connections are links, bonds and relationships among people, objects, organisms or ideas.

In this chapter we are looking at how ideas and people are connected to each other through our opinions and points of view. In times of conflict, we can see how different viewpoints can destroy connections between people and communities. On the other hand, in the stories in this chapter, we saw how a change in point of view can resolve arguments and conflicts, and help to maintain good connections between individuals.

Empathy is being able to connect with other people and understand them. It is an important form of emotional intelligence.

The narrator of the novel *To Kill a Mockingbird* is a young girl called Scout. In Chapter 3 Scout has had a horrible first day at school. Her older brother ignores her, she argues with her teacher, and she embarrasses another boy in her class. That evening she tells her father, Atticus, that she does not want to go back to school because she cannot get on with other people.

Atticus gives his daughter some advice that he hopes will teach her not only to tolerate others, but to show more empathy to them.

> "First of all," he said, "if you can learn a simple trick, Scout, you'll get along a lot better with all kinds of folks. You never really understand a person until you consider things from his point of view—"
>
> "Sir?"
>
> "—until you climb into his skin and walk around in it."

What does Atticus mean by this statement?

How do Atticus' words help Scout, and us, to understand the meaning of empathy?

Thinking about connections and empathy

Look at the picture. In it there is a clear lack of empathy for the boy in the foreground.

In groups discuss these questions.

A. What is happening?

B. Why it is happening?

C. What advice you would give to the boy?

D. Think about the father's advice to his young daughter, Scout. What advice you would give to the girls in the background?

E. What would you do if you were an observer and if the same situation occurred at your school?

Research and design an anti-bullying poster that emphasizes the need for connections and empathy.

In groups look at the poster. How can empathy help us to connect with other people, particularly those from very different cultures and social backgrounds? What answers can you brainstorm and agree on?

Secondly, read and discuss the verse from the song. The singer is looking for empathy from others.

1 What are the connections between the song lyrics and the poster? How do both media items relate to the idea of empathy?

2 Identify a social issue in your society that could be improved if people from different groups showed more empathy for one another.

3 What event could you create to help the present situation in your society?

4 Work in groups to publicize your event.

Walk a mile in my shoes

If I could be you
And you could be me
For just one hour
If we could find a way
To get inside
Each other's mind,
If you could see you
Through your eyes
Instead of your ego
I believe you'd be
Surprised to see
That you'd been blind,
Walk a mile in my shoes
Walk a mile in my shoes
Hey, before you abuse,
criticize and accuse
Walk a mile in my shoes
Joe South

What happens when we use force to solve our problems?

Conceptual question

Before you read Text C

Criteria 3Bi, 3Biii

What problems cause the worst arguments among friends?

Here is a list of the top 16 reasons for arguments amongst friends and families:

1. Blaming someone, or them blaming you
2. Holding different opinions/points of view/values
3. Disagreeing about how to do something
4. Fighting over the same thing (over-competitiveness)
5. Inconsiderate/unfair behaviour
6. Jealousy
7. Lack of empathy/understanding
8. Lack of trust
9. Not having the same background
10. Only one person can win (win–lose)
11. Prejudice/insults
12. Pressure from outside: friends and family
13. There aren't enough resources to share (scarcity)
14. There isn't enough money (poverty)
15. Wanting to do different things
16. Wanting to do the same things differently

Ask yourself:

- Which six of these issues cause the most arguments between friends?

- Which six reasons for arguments are most common in families?

Compare and discuss your answers in groups or in class and create a list you can all agree on.

ATL Social and thinking skills

Here are ten ways of managing conflict.

1. Being fair and equitable when sharing.
2. Encouraging the other person to express an opinion.
3. Exercising leadership.
4. Giving meaningful advice.
5. Listening actively to the other person.
6. Practising empathy.
7. Standing up for your own rights and needs.
8. Taking responsibility for your own actions.
9. Using social media to develop a relationship.
10. Working collaboratively to find areas of agreement.

In groups choose the five best ways of managing a conflict between friends. Justify your answers.

Criteria 3Bi, 3Bii

While you read Text C

The story you are about to read is a fable. It tells the story of a very unhappy marriage. In it are six characters. In alphabetical order they are:

the baron   the boatman   the lover

the baroness   the friend   the gatekeeper.

As you read, identify the motives of the six characters. What makes each one act in the way that they do?

Warning: This story has no happy ending.

Text C

The Drawbridge

As he left for a visit to his outlying districts, the jealous Baron warned his pretty wife: "Do not leave the castle while I am gone, or I will punish you severely when I return!"

But as the hours passed, the young Baroness grew lonely, and despite her husband's warning, decided to visit her Lover who lived in the countryside nearby. The castle was located on an island in a wide, fast flowing river, with a drawbridge linking the island and the land at the narrowest point in the river.

"Surely my husband will not return before dawn," she thought, and ordered the servants to lower the drawbridge and leave it down until she returned.

After spending several pleasant hours with her Lover, the Baroness returned to the drawbridge, only to find it blocked by a Gatekeeper wildly waving a long and extremely sharp knife.

"Do not attempt to cross this bridge, Baroness. If you attempt to do so, I have orders from the Baron to kill you," he said. Fearing for her life, the Baroness returned to her lover and asked him to help.

"Our relationship is only a romantic one," he said, "I will not help." The Baroness then sought out a Boatman on the river, explained her plight to him, and asked him to take her across the river in his boat.

"I will do it, but only if you can pay my fee of five Marks."

"But I have no money with me!" the Baroness protested.

"That is too bad. No, money, no ride," the Boatman said flatly.

Her fear growing, the Baroness ran crying to the home of a Friend, and after again explaining the situation, begged for enough money to pay the Boatman his fee.

"If you had not disobeyed your husband, this would not have happened," the Friend said. "I will give you no money."

With dawn approaching and her last resource exhausted, the Baroness returned to the bridge in desperation, attempted to cross to the castle, and was killed by the Gatekeeper.

Judith H. Katz. 1978. *White Awareness: Handbook for Anti-Racism Training.* University of Oklahoma. pp. 70–72. (adapted)

After you read Text C

After a first reading of the text, copy and fill in the table by yourself. Do not discuss your ideas yet. You will have plenty of opportunities to share your ideas later.

Rank the characters' responsibility for the baroness's death. Who is the most responsible? Who is the least responsible? Give reasons for your answers.

Most responsible	Character	Reasons and justifications for your answers
1.		
2.		
3.		
4.		
5.		
6.		
Least responsible		

Text handling: Text C

Criteria 3Bi, 3Bii

① Factual assessment of Text C

In groups discuss the answers to the following questions. Record your answers. Be prepared to discuss your choices in a whole-class activity.

1. How much did the lover really care for the baroness?
   A. A lot
   B. Not at all
   C. Only when it suited
   D. Passionately ☐
   Justifications/evidence:

2. Which person put morality before friendship?
   A. The baron
   B. The boatman
   C. The lover
   D. The friend ☐
   Justifications/evidence:

3. The boatman asked for money because he was:
    A. greedy
    B. afraid
    C. jealous
    D. angry.
    Justifications/evidence:

4. The gatekeeper obeyed the baron's order to kill
    because he was:
    A. vicious
    B. afraid
    C. unthinking
    D. angry.
    Justifications/evidence:

5. The baron gave the terrible order to the boatman
    because he was:
    A. bloodthirsty
    B. afraid
    C. jealous
    D. a bully.
    Justifications/evidence:

6. Who has all the political power in the story?
    A. The baron
    B. The boatman
    C. The lover
    D. The friend
    Justifications/evidence:

7. The baron's laws are:
    A. fair and just
    B. democratic
    C. unfair and unjust
    D. moral.
    Justifications/evidence:

8. In the fable the baroness died because:
    A. she disobeyed her husband
    B. she was a victim of her husband's oppression
    C. some people were more interested in money
    D. some people were more interested in morality
    E. some people were afraid to speak out against
        the powerful.
    F. All, some or none of the above.
    Justifications/evidence:

Planning and scaffolding

After your discussions, fill in the chart a second time to show who you now think is responsible for the baroness's death. Again give reasons for your answers.

Most responsible	Character	Reasons and justifications for your answers
1.		
2.		
3.		
4.		
5.		
6.		
Least responsible		

ATL Thinking skills

Criterion 3Biii

Now that you have answered questions 1–8, do you still have the same ideas about the characters' actions?

In what ways have your ideas and perspectives changed?

Discussion and debate

Look at the poster on the right and think about the story you have just read.

- How does the poster help us to understand the real message of "The Drawbridge"?
- In what ways does it speak about the right and wrong ways of solving conflict?
- If we conclude that the baron is a bully, how does this fact change our point of view of the other characters, especially the baroness?
- How much empathy can you feel for the other characters?
- Do you understand the baroness's situation? Can you empathize with her? Be prepared to justify your ideas in a class discussion.

Inspire hope.
Speak out against domestic violence.

Thinking and communication skills

What can you see in the picture below?

A. A young woman

B. An old woman

C. Both

D. Neither

- What does the picture teach us about a point of view? How did your point of view change after you had reread and thought about the story of the baroness and the drawbridge?

- How much have your ideas about the motives of the characters changed in the course of this exercise?

- What does the story teach us about empathy and points of view?

- What does the story teach us about conflict resolution?

Formative interactive oral activity: Speech

Criteria 3Ci, 3Cii, 3Ciii

"The Drawbridge" is a story that is used to teach us **empathy.**

The purpose of this exercise is for you to convince your fellow classmates that the baron and the other characters all acted out of necessity.

Show your empathy for one of the characters in the story. Use the notes from the previous exercises to prepare a speech defending the character's actions.

Your speech should be three or four minutes in length. You may wish to deliver your speech individually, or in a small group.

Planning and scaffolding

You may find it helpful to copy and use this table to help you structure your speech.

My big idea is …	Example: The gatekeeper is/is not totally responsible for the death of the baroness.	
Point/idea/opinion*	Evidence in the story	Example in real life
Reason		
Reason		
Reason		
Reason		
In conclusion I believe (that) …		

Planning and scaffolding

Criterion 3Civ

Communicating with a sense of audience

Now think about the language you will use in the speech. Choose one of these registers:

- very formal, as if talking politely to very important strangers
- formal, as if talking very politely to people you don't know well
- informal, as if talking to a friend.

Self-management skills

Manage your time and your tasks effectively

- Set goals that are challenging and realistic.

- Plan strategies and take action to achieve personal and academic goals.

- Use appropriate strategies for organizing complex information.

- Select and use technology effectively and productively.

Planning and scaffolding

Practise, practise, practise

As we have already seen, one secret of successful public speaking is practice.

Practising what you want to say can be a really useful aid to confidence building and language learning.

Practise what you are going to say with a friend, or with other members of your group.

You can video yourself. You can even practise before a mirror.

Think about what you did well and where you can improve.

Then practise some more.

Formative written activity: Reasoned argument

Criteria 3Di, 3Dii, 3Diii

A "reasoned argument" is a series of statements that use evidence and reasoning to persuade someone to accept or reject a particular opinion.

Use a reasoned argument to answer the question: "Is the baroness responsible for her own death?" Write between 200 and 250 words.

Planning and scaffolding

First decide what your answer to the question is.

This answer will be your "big idea" or thesis.

Write down the points that prove your thesis. In the table below there are some ideas. You may wish to copy the table and use these or you may prefer to use ideas of your own.

For each supporting idea, find evidence in the story and/or find an example from real life.

Come to a conclusion. In your conclusion state what you have learned or make a recommendation.

My thesis is …	The baroness is/is not responsible for her own death.	
Point/idea/opinion*	Evidence in the story	Example in real life
The baroness was in a very unhappy marriage.	Her husband would not let her leave the castle.	Some husbands tell their wives not to leave the house.
The baron is a bully.		
The lover is a coward.		
The friend was not a real friend.		
The boatman cared too much about money.		
The gatekeeper was a coward.		
The whole town was afraid of the baron.		
In conclusion I believe (that) …		

Note: You can change any or all of these opinions to suit your interpretation of the story.

Planning and scaffolding

Criterion 3Diii

Communicating with a sense of audience

The reasoned argument is a piece of writing for your teacher. Think about the language you will use in the reasoned argument. Choose one of these registers:

- very formal, as if talking politely to a very important stranger
- formal, as if talking very politely to people you don't know well
- informal, as if talking to a friend.

Conclusion to the conceptual question

What happens when we use force to solve our problems?

Having examined this section, what is your answer to the question?

What and how does audio-visual Text D communicate about the themes of conflict and resolution?

Before you watch Text D

What do we know so far?

In this chapter you have looked into the topic of conflict resolution. As a class, make a list of the most important ideas you have learned so far in your investigations.

At this stage, are there any points you don't understand?

Make a list of your questions.

How many answers can you find in this audio-visual section?

Suggested texts for this section

A. **In The Mix: Conflict Resolution – Thinking It Through (Excerpt)**

   https://www.youtube.com/watch?v=xDoQIpe5TxA

B. **Bullying, Drama, Conflict Resolution Education for Middle School**

   https://www.youtube.com/watch?v=N2_DSbnQHOQ

C. **Playground Conflict Resolution for younger students**

   https://vimeo.com/78557743

Note: Alternatively, you could use an audio-visual stimulus related to the theme of conflict resolution of your own choosing.

ATL Research skills

Media Literacy

In this section you can develop these valuable 21st century learning skills:

*   Interacting with media to use and create ideas and information.

*   Making informed choices about personal viewing experiences.

*   Understanding the impact of media representations.

*   Seeking a range of perspectives from varied sources.

*   Communicating information and ideas effectively.

Before you watch Text D

Focusing activity

Read through the exercises below to make sure you know what to look and listen for. You may need to watch the materials several times and discuss possible answers in class after each viewing and listening.

While you watch Text D

Criterion: 3Ai

Respond to the tasks and answer the questions in the appropriate manner.

1. 1. This audio-visual stimulus seems to be related to which of these MYP global contexts?
   A. Identities and relationships
   B. Orientation in space and time
   C. Personal and cultural expression
   D. Scientific and technical innovation
   E. Globalization and sustainability
   F. Fairness and development ☐

2. Copy this table and use it to summarize the main points of the stimulus. You may wish to add extra supporting points, if necessary.

	Main idea	Examples and/or explanations and/or details
Subject matter		
Thesis – main point		
Supporting point 1		
Supporting point 2		
Supporting point 3		
Supporting point 4		
Conclusions		

2. **Multiple-choice with justifications**

3. The approach to the subject matter of the audio-visual stimulus is mainly:
   A. entertaining
   B. factual
   C. persuasive
   D. other. ☐
   Justification/reason:

4. How would you describe the content of the stimulus?
   A. Really interesting
   B. Interesting
   C. Fairly interesting
   D. Uninteresting ☐
   Justification/reason:

3 **Multiple-choice questions**

5. What was the format of the audio-visual stimulus?
   A. Speech
   B. Conversation/discussion
   C. Debate
   D. Documentary
   E. Other ☐

6. The purpose of the audio-visual stimulus was to:
   A. narrate a story
   B. describe a situation
   C. explain a problem
   D. argue a point of view
   E. give instructions/ guidelines
   F. other (please specify) ☐

7. How many points of view did the audio-visual stimulus show?
   A. One
   B. Two
   C. Three
   D. More than three ☐

8. The opinions in the audio-visual stimulus are:
   A. very balanced
   B. quite balanced
   C. biased
   D. very one-sided. ☐

9. How much did the audio-visual stimulus use graphics?
   A. A lot
   B. More than twice
   C. Once or twice
   D. Never ☐

10. Which of these techniques are used in the audio-visual stimulus?
    A. Voiceover
    B. Special lighting techniques
    C. Music and sound effects
    D. Other special effects
    E. None of the above
    F. All of the above
    G. Some of the above (please specify) ☐

Formative writing activity: Reasoned argument

Criterion 3Aiii

Summarize the main points of the audio-video stimulus you have watched in the form of a reasoned argument. You may wish to use information from question 2.

Remember to use paragraphing and linking words to communicate your argument clearly.

Subject matter		
Thesis – main point		
Supporting point 1		Example/Evidence:
Supporting point 2		Example/Evidence:
Supporting point 3		Example/Evidence:
Conclusion		

Formative interactive oral: Speech

Criterion 3Aiii

Imagine you have been asked to speak to the rest of your class on the issue of conflict resolution. You will deliver a speech either agreeing or disagreeing with the content of the video you have watched.

First of all, in groups decide whether you agree or disagree with the ideas themselves. You will have already collected most of this information when you completed your reasoned argument above. Now add your own opinions and reasons. Use the chart below to help you plan your speech.

Subject matter of the video			
Thesis – main point of the video			
		Your opinions	Reasons and justifications
Supporting point 1		Agree/disagree	
Supporting point 2		Agree/disagree	
Supporting point 3		Agree/disagree	
Conclusions			

Self-management skills

Consider the process of learning

Develop new skills, techniques and strategies for effective learning.

Identify strengths and weaknesses of personal learning strategies.

Consider your communication and speech-giving skills

Ask yourself:

- How can I improve a specific skill?
- What can I already do?
- What will I work on next?

Consider personal learning strategies

Ask yourself:

- What can I do to become a more efficient and effective learner?

In this instance, you could focus on the process of creating your own work by imitating the ideas in this chapter.

Ask yourself:

- What else can I do to help myself?

Planning and scaffolding   Criterion 3Civ

Communicating with a sense of audience

Now think about the language you will use in the speech. Who is your audience? How serious is the topic? Choose one of these registers:

- very formal, as if talking politely to a very important stranger
- formal, as if talking very politely to people you don't know well
- informal, as if talking to a friend.

Planning and scaffolding

Now use and adapt the material to prepare a speech to your audience.

Look at the notes in this chapter on preparing and giving a speech.

Present your speech. You can do this in front of your class, or you could record yourself and share the recording with your teacher and/or the class.

Research and self-management skills

Have you found answers to all the questions you asked at the beginning of this section? If not, where, and how, do you think you could find the information you are seeking?

Conclusion to the conceptual question

What and how does audio-visual Text D communicate about the themes of conflict and resolution?

Having examined this section, what is your answer to the question?

Summative activities

In this summative assessment you will have an opportunity to show your understanding of the topic of conflict resolution and the statement of inquiry. You will also be assessed on your use of the communication skills you have developed in this chapter.

To complete the assessment you will undertake two tasks. Each task requires you to answer a debatable question.

Statement of inquiry

Stories are almost always about conflict. They connect cultures by describing the universal ways and means of resolving personal and global differences.

Debatable question 1

Is conflict avoidable?

Debatable question 2

Can a story teach us how to solve a conflict?

For the first task you will watch a video and produce a speech based on the content. To answer the second question, you will have to read two texts and produce a reasoned argument based on the contents.

Summative oral task: Speech

Watch the following video entitled "Conflict resolution" by Australian business coach, Jeff Muir. Alternatively, watch a video on a related subject of your own choosing. Make notes to help you to answer the debatable question:

Debatable question 1 Is conflict avoidable?

Using evidence/examples from the words and images from the video, create and make a speech of 3–4 minutes' duration to respond to the debatable question. You may wish to record your speech.

You have had opportunities to practise and undertake speeches throughout this unit. In this summative assessment you will have a final opportunity to show your understanding of the following learning objectives:

A: Comprehending spoken and visual text

3Ai	*Show understanding of information, main ideas and supporting details, and draw conclusions*
3Aii	*Understand conventions*
3Aiii	*Engage with the spoken and visual text by identifying ideas, opinions and attitudes and by making a response to the text based on personal experiences and opinions*

C: Communicating in response to spoken and/or written and/or visual text

3Ci	*Respond appropriately to spoken and/or written and/or visual text*
3Cii	*Interact in rehearsed and unrehearsed exchanges*
3Ciii	*Express ideas and feelings, and communicate information in familiar and some unfamiliar situations*
3Civ	*Communicate with a sense of audience and purpose*

D: Using language in spoken and/or written form

3Di	*Write and/or speak using a range of vocabulary, grammatical structures and conventions; when speaking, use clear pronunciation and intonation*
3Dii	*Organize information and ideas and use a range of basic cohesive devices*
3Diii	*Use language to suit the context*

Text E

"Conflict resolution"

This is a conflict resolution lecture for business people, with cartoons.

https://www.youtube.com/watch?v=KY5TWVz5ZDU

Summative written task: Reasoned argument

Read the following story (Text F).

Based on the information you read in Texts F, write a reasoned argument to answer this debatable question:

Debatable question 2   Can a story teach us how to solve a conflict?

Your reasoned argument should set out your thesis, have three or four supporting points and come to a clear conclusion. Use cohesive devices to link your ideas.

Write 200–250 words.

You have had opportunities to practise and write reasoned arguments throughout this unit. In this summative assessment you will have a final opportunity to show your understanding of the following learning objectives:

B: Comprehending written and visual text

3Bi	*Show understanding of information, main ideas and supporting details, and draw conclusions*
3Bii	*Understand basic conventions including aspects of format and style, and author's purpose for writing*
3Biii	*Engage with the written and visual text by identifying ideas, opinions and attitudes and by making a response to the text based on personal experiences and opinions*

C: Communicating in response to spoken and/or written and/or visual text

3Ci	*Respond appropriately to spoken and/or written and/or visual text*
3Cii	*Interact in rehearsed and unrehearsed exchanges*
3Ciii	*Express ideas and feelings, and communicate information in familiar and some unfamiliar situations*
3Civ	*Communicate with a sense of audience and purpose*

D: Using language in spoken and/or written form

3Di	*Write and/or speak using a range of vocabulary, grammatical structures and conventions; when speaking, use clear pronunciation and intonation*
3Dii	*Organize information and ideas and use a range of basic cohesive devices*
3Diii	*Use language to suit the context*

The poor fisherman, the genie and the teacher

Once upon a time, there lived a poor fisherman. Being poor was bad but what really made him sad was the fact that he and his wife had no children. Poor parents could hope that their children would care for them in their old age. The fisherman lived with his wife and his blind old mother. Unfortunately, his wife and his blind old mother argued all the time.

At the end of one particularly long, fishless day, the fisherman found a small bottle in his net. It was old and shabby but the fisherman thought to himself that perhaps he could clean it and he would be able to sell it. He pulled out the stopper, and there was a flash of light and then a pillar of smoke rose out of the bottle.

The pillar of smoke formed into the shape of a genie who cried "Free! I'm free at last!" The genie explained that he had been imprisoned in the bottle for 1,000 years.

The genie was so pleased to be free that he offered to grant the

fisherman one single wish. The fisherman thought about his childless wife. Then he thought about his blind mother. He asked the genie if he could go home and ask his wife and his mother what the wish should be. The genie agreed and told the fisherman to come back to the same spot at the same time next week.

Excited, the fisherman rushed home and told his mother what had happened. She said to him "My son, I have been blind for decades. You must ask the genie to give me my sight."

Shortly after that, the poor fisherman's wife returned. He told her what had happened and what his mother had said. "How typically selfish of your mother!" cried his wife. "Take no notice of her. Ask the genie for a son, that we may have a child, and someone to care for us in our old age."

The fisherman could not think of a way to meet the wishes of both his mother and his wife. As the week went on his wife and his mother argued incessantly between themselves. On occasions, they almost came to blows. At the end of the week, the poor fisherman still did not know what to do.

In desperation, the fisherman took his wife and mother to see the teacher. He gave the teacher his last fish and told the teacher his story. But when he had finished, his wife and mother began to argue again. The teacher listened carefully and then replied:

"You must return to the genie, and you must honour the wishes of both your wife and your mother."

"But how does this help?" cried the poor fisherman, his blind old mother and his wife together. "The genie will grant only one wish!"

The teacher whispered something in the poor fisherman's ear.

The next day, the poor fisherman went to the spot where he had found the genie and sure enough, the genie appeared, and offered to grant him one wish.

"Genie," said the poor fisherman, "I ask nothing for myself, and my wife asks nothing for herself. But we respect our parents and elders. It is the duty of all children. So I ask on behalf of my aged mother that you grant her one wish before she dies."

"You are a good son," said the genie, "I will grant your aged mother's wish. What does she wish for?"

"My aged mother's one wish, O genie, is that she might see her grandson before she dies."

Adapted from: https://mythologystories.wordpress.com/2013/12/27/1001nights-4/

Going beyond the chapter

In this chapter you have explored how stories can illustrate conflict. These tales connect different cultures by describing universal ways and means of resolving personal and global differences.

Now make use of the information you have learned and the communication skills you have developed in this chapter for practical purposes beyond the classroom.

Take Action! Some suggestions ...

Write a short story

Having learned about conflicts in both stories and in real life, write a story that includes one or more conflicts. All stories contain at least one or more of the following types of conflicts:

- Character versus character (such as a hero versus a villain)

- Character versus self (where a character has to get over something inside themselves like lack of confidence)

- Character versus society (where a character, alone or with others, challenges the way a society is)

- Character versus nature (where a character is challenged by a force of nature such as snow storms, or has to survive somewhere like an island or the desert)

- Think about what the message or theme of your story is going to be. How will the character(s) solve the conflict? What will the message be for the reader?

Join a debating club or society

If you enjoyed carrying out the speech and/or the reasoned argument tasks in this chapter, you might consider joining a debating club or society. If there is none in your school or local community, you might consider starting one in your school!

Service learning

Speak to your MYP coordinator or action and service coordinator to find out your school's expectations for action and service in your particular grade/year.

The ideas below relate directly to the following service learning outcomes:

- become more aware of their own strengths and areas for growth
- undertake challenges that develop new skills
- discuss, evaluate and plan student-initiated activities
- persevere in action
- work collaboratively with others
- develop international-mindedness through global engagement, multilingualism and intercultural understanding
- consider the ethical implications of their actions.

Ideas for service

Create a video that can be used by teachers to teach MYP students about conflict and how students can solve conflicts. Use the information you have read about and researched in this chapter, such as the top 16 reasons for arguments among friends. You could base your video on the conflict resolution video you watched in this chapter, but adapt it for a student audience instead.

Get in contact with local community groups, charities or NGOs to find out if they run something similar to the "Walk A Mile In My Shoes" campaign and get you and your school involved. If there are no such events planned, why not run your own similar event?

If you enjoyed this chapter here are some texts on conflict resolution for further reading

- Stephen Chbosky, *The Perks of Being a Wallflower*
- John Green, *The Fault in Our Stars*
- John Green, *Looking for Alaska*
- Laurie Halse Anderson, *Speak*
- S.E. Hinton, *The Outsiders*
- Harper Lee, *To Kill a Mockingbird*

ATL Research and thinking skills

At the end of any learning experience always ask yourself these questions:

- What lessons have I learned from this chapter?
- What concepts don't I yet understand about this topic?
- What questions do I still have about this topic?
- Where can I find answers to these questions?

4 Abilities and opportunities

In context

Global context: Personal and cultural expression

What is the nature and purpose of creative expression?

In this chapter we are exploring the ways in which we can assess our situation, use our abilities, make the most of opportunities, overcome difficulties and achieve our ambitions. We will also look at ways we can use our skills and talents to make a difference to others.

Key concept

Connections are links, bonds and relationships between people, objects, organisms or ideas. In this chapter we think about how people are connected to the societies in which they live. We will look at the idea of "needs" and think about how people overcome social and personal difficulties, such as poverty and low self-esteem.

Connections are also central to the study of language. Language connects us to other people. In Language Acquisition we have to think about the relationships between speaker and audience, writer and reader.

Related concept

Messages are the information speakers and writers communicate with their audience.

Statement of inquiry

We can use language to describe and realize our personal ambitions and abilities and, having done so, define ways in which we can use our abilities to help others.

Inquiry questions

→ What made Michael Oher's dreams come true?

→ How difficult is it to achieve our ambitions?

→ How can we use our skills to help others?

→ How does audio-visual Text D communicate the theme of personal development?

→ Can service learning help you to develop your own skills and enable you to help others?

→ Do we have to make the most of our opportunities before we can make the most of our abilities?

What made Michael Oher's dreams come true?

Before you read Text A

Criteria: 3Ci, 3Cii, 3Ciii

Discussion: What do we need for a good life?

What do you know about themes of abilities and opportunities? How are the two ideas connected?

Before you begin this chapter, conduct a class brainstorming session. You could start by asking, "Are our opportunities limited by our abilities?"

In this chapter we are going to look at what people need to become successful in life. Think about the different needs we all have. Here is a list of "things" we need or want in life. Can you add to the list?

Health: the need to be well

Security: feeling safe from danger

Belonging: the need for loving, sharing, and fitting in with others

Esteem: the need for feeling important and being respected

Learning: the need to make choices and decisions

Fun: the need for being happy, and finding joy in life

ATL Social and communication skills

On the exercises on this page use your social skills to work effectively with others.

- Work collaboratively in a team.
- Work towards agreement.
- Help others to succeed.
- Encourage others to contribute.

Discussion and debate

- Compare the two pictures of the beggar and the happy family.
- What do the two pictures tell us in terms of different people's needs and achievements?
- Describe the two pictures in terms of what the people in them "have" and "have not" and what they have achieved or not achieved in life?
- Create a caption for each picture to explain the message of each. Create a further title to communicate the meaning of the two pictures together.

Think about the needs and ambitions of young people of your generation. Make a list of things you have and things you will need to achieve your ambitions. Discuss your lists in class.

Before and while you read Text A

Predicting the content of the text

Text A is the biography of Michael Oher, who was born in poverty but became a very successful American football player. He was the subject of the Hollywood film *The Blind Side*.

Look at the eight statements about abilities and opportunities below. Before you read, decide whether the statements are generally true, untrue or partially true. Note your answers in the left-hand column.

While you read the text, decide whether each sentence is true, untrue or partially true in the case of Michael Oher. Note your answers in the right-hand column, "In Michael's case".

In the far right column "Proof from the text", give evidence from the text to back up your answers.

In general: true/untrue/ probably true	Eight statements about abilities and opportunities	In Michael's case: true/untrue/ probably true	Proof from the text
	A child born into a poor family might not have important learning skills.		
	Poverty and a lack of safety can lead to poor health and social problems.		
	Unhealthy and stressed children are less likely to succeed at school.		
	Poor children have very poor social skills at school.		
	Children with big problems can learn if they are cared for.		
	Successes in one area can help a child to find self-esteem.		
	Greater self-esteem leads to greater success in other areas of life.		
	Poor children are not likely to become successful adults.		

https://en.wikipedia.org/wiki/Michael_Oher

The Story of Michael Oher

Michael Oher was born on May 28, 1986 in Memphis, Tennessee. He was one of twelve children. His mother was an alcoholic and crack cocaine addict and his father was frequently in prison. Michael received little attention and discipline during his childhood.

In school Michael had to repeat both first and second grades. He was placed in foster care at age seven. After that he lived in various foster homes and was often homeless. Michael attended eleven different schools during his first nine years as a student.

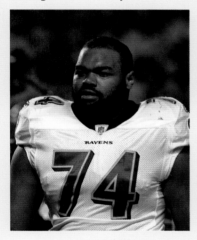

By the time he was a 16-year-old student, Michael's academic grades were still very poor. He was sleeping on people's couches and carried his belongings in a few plastic bags. However, in his junior year at a public high school in Memphis, he began to excel at football.

With the help of Tony Henderson, an auto mechanic, with whom he was living temporarily, the 16 year old applied for admission to Briarcrest Christian School. The headmaster agreed to accept Michael because of his sporting skills.

One morning, businesswoman Leigh Anne Tuohy was driving along a Memphis street with her husband, Sean, and their two children. She noticed Michael, who was easy to spot because he was already 1.96 metres tall. But that freezing cold day he was only wearing shorts and a T-shirt.

The children, Collins and S.J., recognised Michael, who was their classmate at school. He was by far the biggest student at school and one of few African-Americans.

The Tuohy family made room for Michael in their car. "It was nothing and everything," Leigh Anne says. "It was just one of those things that you should do."

The family began to help Michael. At first, they let him sleep on their couch. Eventually, Leigh Anne gave him a bedroom and bought him a bed. He later told her this was the first bed he ever had.

Over time, Michael became a much-loved member of the family and the Tuohys became his legal guardians when the boy was 17, and eventually adopted him.

The parents hired a tutor for Michael to work with him for 20 hours per week. The young man also took 10-day-long internet-based courses from Brigham Young University. Taking and passing the Internet courses allowed him to replace his very low marks with A grades.

Michael was, of course, also playing football for his junior year. His size, quickness and protective nature helped him to become one of the best high school football players in the country. He quickly became a top junior footballer in the state of Tennessee, which led to multiple scholarship offers from major universities.

He ultimately chose to play college football at the University of Mississippi. He later became a very successful professional player with the Baltimore Ravens, the Tennessee Titans and the Carolina Panthers.

As word of his story spread, author Michael Lewis wrote about Michael's journey from homeless teen to star athlete. His book, *The Blind Side: Evolution of a Game*, became a *New York Times* bestseller. Michael's story with the Tuohy family was also told in the Academy Award-winning 2009 film *The Blind Side*, starring Sandra Bullock and Tim McGraw.

Sources: http://www.oprah.com/entertainment/ Michael-Ohers-Inspiring-Journey-The-Blind-Side; https://en.wikipedia.org/wiki/Michael_Oher

Text handling: Factual assessment of Text A

Criterion: 3Bi

1 True/false with justification

Read the text carefully and identify which of the statements below are true and which are false. Justify each answer with a relevant brief quotation from the text. Write your answers on a separate sheet of paper. Both a correct identification and a quotation are required for one mark.

		True	False
Example:	Michael had eleven siblings.	✓	
Justification	"He was one of twelve children"		
1	Michael's parents took good care of him when he was a little child.		
Justification:			
2	He was very poor learner in elementary school.		
Justification:			
3	Although Michael lacked a stable home life he stayed on at school.		
Justification:			
4	At 16 he passed an exam to go to Briarcrest Christian School.		
Justification:			
5	The Tuohy family gave Michael the domestic stability he had never had.		
Justification:			
6	The Tuohys treated Michael like a son.		
Justification:			
7	Michael always worked independently to improve his academic scores.		
Justification:			
8	He became a professional footballer while he was still at school.		
Justification:			

2 Multiple-choice questions

Choose the correct answer from A, B, C, or D. Write the letter in the answer box provided.

9. In the first 16 years Michael went without:
    A. attending school
    B. playing football
    C. a proper place to live
    D. good health.

10. Until meeting the Tuohy family Michael did badly at school because:
    A. he was a poor student
    B. he could not read or write
    C. he lacked a proper family life
    D. he was not interested in school.

11. As well as safety and stability Michael also found:
    A. financial success
    B. quick academic success
    C. a sense of belonging to a real family
    D. a sense of independence.

12. Michael was able to improve his school grades because of:
    A. tutoring and hard work
    B. his footballing skills
    C. extra help from his school
    D. his kind and friendly personality.

3 Short-answer questions

Answer the following questions:

13. What three qualities allowed Michael to become an excellent football player?

14. Which phrase tells us that Michael had offers from many universities?

15. Which phrase explains why the author Michael Lewis wanted to write a book about Michael Oher?

16. Summarize the different ways in which the Tuohys assisted and supported Michael?

Discussion and debate

In conclusion, explain how and why Michael was able to successfully follow his dreams of becoming a great footballer. Justify your answers by evaluating the evidence in the text and drawing reasonable conclusions.

ATL Communication skills

You could work on the questions in pairs.

- Preview and skim the text to build understanding.
- Read it critically for comprehension.
- Make inferences and draw conclusions.
- Paraphrase accurately and concisely.

Formative oral and interactive skills

Discussion

Could Michael Oher have become a successful sportsman without the support of a family?

In groups discuss the question above.

Planning and scaffolding

Criteria 3Civ

First read the eight statements below about the connections between poverty and success. In your groups choose three of these statements that you think are most relevant to Michael. You may also wish to come to a different conclusion to those on the list. Give reasons for your answers.

1. A child born into a poor family might not have important learning skills.
2. Poverty and a lack of safety can lead to poor health and social problems.
3. Unhealthy and stressed children are less likely to succeed at school.
4. Poor children have very poor social skills at school.
5. Children with big problems can learn if they are cared for.
6. Successes in one area can help a child to find self-esteem.
7. Greater self-esteem leads to greater success in other areas of life.
8. Poor children are not likely to become successful adults.
9. Our alternative conclusion is …

During the discussion you should listen to everyone's point of view and then come to an agreed conclusion.

The purpose of the exercise is to find answers that everyone in the group can all agree with.

Present your findings to the rest of the class using clear formal English.

Planning and scaffolding

Criterion 3Civ

Communicating with a sense of audience

Now think about the language you will use in the discussion. Who are you speaking with? Choose one of these registers:

- very formal, as if talking politely to a very important stranger
- formal, as if talking very politely to people you don't know well
- informal, as if talking to a friend.

ATL Thinking skills

Use your critical thinking skills as your groups works on these exercises.

- Analyse and evaluate issues and ideas.
- Gather and organize relevant information to formulate an argument.
- Interpret data.
- Evaluate evidence and arguments.
- Draw reasonable conclusions.
- Test your conclusions.
- Revise your understandings based on new information and evidence.

Formative writing skills – Description

Criteria: 3Di, 3Dii, 3Diii

Imagine you are one of Michael Oher's classmates. Write a description of 16-year-old Michael and his ambitions to be a great sportsman. Use the text and the pictures in this section to help you. You could put your thoughts into a letter to a friend, a diary entry, or blog. Write between 200 and 250 words.

Description	Things you know
His background	
His appearance	
His actions and behaviour	
The reaction of people around him • Teachers • Classmates • The Tuohy family	
His motives and ambitions • School subjects • Sports	

Planning and scaffolding

Use the chart opposite and use it to help you gather your ideas. Describe what you know about the young man.

Planning and scaffolding

Criterion 3Diii

Communicating with a sense of audience

Now think about the language you will use in your text. Who are you writing to? Choose one of these registers:

• very formal, as if talking politely to a very important stranger
• formal, as if talking very politely to people you don't know well
• informal, as if talking to a friend.

Conclusion to factual question

What made Michael Oher's dreams come true?

Was it Michael's abilities or his opportunities that changed his life? Having examined this section, what is your answer to the question?

How difficult is it to achieve our ambitions?

Conceptual question

Before you read Text B

Criteria: 3Biii, 3Ciii

Children who grow up in poverty, like the young Michael Oher, have to overcome a huge number of barriers to success. Here is a list of such problems.

In groups rank all these problems on a scale of 1–5 and discuss. Choose the five problems you think are the most important barriers to success. Share your results with the class.

Life's problems

- Being cold
- Few chances to succeed
- Few opportunities to succeed
- Friendlessness
- Homelessness
- Hopelessness
- Illness
- Inadequate clothing
- Insecurity
- Lack of ambition
- Low self-esteem
- No job opportunities
- No family
- No sense of being wanted
- No sense of future
- Poor school grades
- Poverty

ATL Thinking and communication skills

Discuss the picture below. In groups imagine what might have happened to the boy to make him become homeless. Share your ideas with the class.

Here is an opportunity to use your creative thinking skills. Ask yourself a series of questions about the boy. Make a list. Answer your own questions. Make guesses. Be inventive.

When you have finished create a diagram in order to convey your findings. Think about the techniques you can use so that the diagram communicates your ideas clearly and effectively.

While you read Text B

Matching parts of a text

In the text below there are five paragraphs marked A–E. Here are eight headings. Discuss the headings with your teacher to check you understand each one.

Match five of the headings to paragraphs A–E.

- Safety needs
- Esteem needs and the need to understand
- Health matters
- Biological and physiological needs
- Self-actualization
- Economic needs
- The need for love and belonging
- Educational needs

Text B

Maslow's hierarchy of needs

How well can a hungry child learn? What happens to a learner who is in danger? How do we unlock our talents and find what we are good at and what we want to be? By asking questions like these, American psychologist Abraham Maslow looked for reasons why some children in need find it difficult to do well at school.

Maslow wondered what motivates children to learn. He thought that we have certain basic needs, which we must fulfil so that we can become successful learners.

Maslow said that we have different types and levels of need that we want to fulfil. He thought that as we fulfil one need, we can move on to a higher one. He called the system a hierarchy of needs.

Everyone is capable and has the desire to move up the hierarchy. Unfortunately, a child's negative life experiences, such as poverty, violence, insecurity and homelessness may stop children moving up through the hierarchy, or cause them to move down a level.

A

We all need air, food, drink, warmth and sleep. Maslow argued that we must satisfy these biological needs before we can learn anything. If we are sick, then little else matters. All children at school must be properly fed and in good health in order to learn well.

B

Maslow realized that poverty is a major problem and we need to be protected and free from fear. We all need a roof over our heads to protect us from the weather and we need to keep ourselves safe from harm. In other words, a child's safety is essential to effective learning. A child can experience domestic violence, criminal activity, or even war. Even in peaceful societies a child who is being victimized or bullied will be prevented from learning.

C

We need positive relationships with family, friends and partners. These relationships give us friendship, affection and love. Maslow recognized that these positive relationships can positively affect a child's future. If people are helpful and kind to us, we can learn from them easily. If the family has high hopes for a child, that child is more likely to do well at school.

D

Children with a positive self-image and confidence tend to do well at school. Self-esteem leads to personal motivation and ambition. If we gain a higher position within a group, people respect us and we have greater power. Children who are neglected may not develop a positive

self-image essential to education. Esteem allows us develop the need to understand. We can develop the confidence to do well when faced with a problem to solve or a challenge to overcome. As the need to understand develops, we may develop aesthetic needs in fields such as art, music, theatre, and dance.

E

Success lets us know what we want to become. We need to set and achieve these personal goals. Success in achieving our goals and ambitions gives us a sense of personal, emotional and professional satisfaction. Self-actualized people know how to express themselves clearly.

Maslow also thought that there was a stage beyond this called Transcendence. Such people go beyond material needs and seek peace with the world. They are loving and creative, realistic and productive. Such people can be independent, spontaneous and playful. They may well have a love for the human race.

Adapted from http://www.ship.edu/~cgboeree/maslow.html

Text handling: Factual meaning of Text B

Criterion 3Bi

1 **Short-answer questions**

Read the first four paragraphs and answer the following questions:

1. What question did Maslow want to answer?
2. What answer did he come to?
3. What happens when we fulfil one need?
4. Why did Maslow call the system he invented a "hierarchy"?
5. What short phrase describes the major problems we can face?

2 **Multiple-choice questions**

Read the rest of the text and choose the correct answer from A, B, C, or D.

6. Maslow said that hunger:
   A. prevents learning   C. does not matter
   B. makes learning difficult   D. makes us learn well.   ☐

7. According to Text B safety needs to include protection from:
   - **A.** danger, hunger and violence
   - **B.** violence, war and thirst
   - **C.** sleep, hunger and warmth
   - **D.** violence, bad weather and danger.

8. According to paragraph C, our need to belong to a family and to a group:
   - **A.** help us to learn from others
   - **B.** make us ambitious
   - **C.** give us good friends
   - **D.** give us a good future.

9. According to paragraph D, if we have high self-esteem we can:
   - **A.** make friends easily
   - **B.** understand our lessons without difficulty
   - **C.** deal with difficulties
   - **D.** tell the difference between right and wrong.

10. According to paragraph E, self-actualization means:
    - **A.** we can become high earners
    - **B.** we can achieve our personal goals
    - **C.** we will be self-satisfied
    - **D.** we can do any job we want.

11. According to paragraph E, transcendence involves:
    - **A.** travelling the world
    - **B.** trying to make the world a better place
    - **C.** being childish
    - **D.** knowing more than everyone else.

ATL Thinking and communication skills   Criteria: 3Bii, 3Biii

Look at this chart of Maslow's hierarchy of needs and in groups discuss the questions that follow.

12. How does the graphic help us to understand Maslow's ideas? List at least five specific techniques. Here are some visual techniques you may want to consider:

   - Colour coding
   - Headings
   - Repetition
   - Body language
   - Structure/composition
   - Symbols
   - Slogans

13. In your opinion, how useful are the ideas and concepts in Maslow's hierarchy? Do they help you to understand your own way in life?

14. Evaluate the graphical text by listing:
   - three things you like about the graphic
   - three improvements you would make.

MORALITY, CREATIVITY, SPONTANEITY, PROBLEM SOLVING, LACK OF PREJUDICE, ACCEPTANCE OF FACTS

SELF-ACTUALIZATION

SELF-ESTEEM, CONFIDENCE, ACHIEVEMENT, RESPECT OF OTHERS, RESPECT BY OTHERS

ESTEEM

FRIENDSHIP, FAMILY, INTIMACY

LOVE/BELONGING

SECURITY OF BODY, OF EMPLOYMENT, OF RESOURCES, OF MORALITY, OF THE FAMILY, OF HELATH, OF PROPERTY

SAFETY

BREATHING, FOOD, WATER, SLEEP

PHYSIOLOGICAL

Oral and interactive skills: Criteria: 3Bi, 3Bii, 3Biii
Discussion

Look at the Cambodian family in the picture below. They are rice farmers. They are a close family but they seem to have little chance of improving their lives. The parents want their children, Thyda (13), Vuth (11) and the baby girl Sreylin to achieve their ambitions, to have good jobs and happy families.

In your group, discuss:

- the main ideas in the graphic
- the audience for the graphic (where "in real life" might the graphic be found?)
- the purpose of the graphic (how is the audience supposed to respond?).

Further discussion

Criteria: 3Ci, 3Cii, 3Ciii

The title of this chapter is Abilities and Opportunities.

All children have abilities. But not every poor child has the same opportunities as Michael Oher.

How do you think children such as Vuth and Puthyda might achieve their dreams?

Discuss ways in which local governments could improve:

A. the basic health needs of children

B. their safety needs

C. their esteem and educational needs.

How can we give children the opportunities to develop their abilities to the fullest?

How can we help children to move up through Maslow's hierarchy?

	Actions	Reasons
Basic health needs		
Safety needs		
Esteem and education needs		
Achievement of ambitions		

Formative writing activity [Criteria 3Di, 3Dii, 3Diii]

Write a description of 200 to 250 words of one of the Cambodian children, Thyda, Vuth or Sreylin, from the exercise above. Describe the child, and his or her ambitions and hopes for the future. Use the results of the discussion above to help you. You could put your thoughts into a letter to a friend, a diary entry or blog.

Planning and scaffolding

You may want to complete the chart below to help you gather your ideas. You may choose to use all or only some of the ideas. Write between 200 and 250 words.

Description	Things you imagine
Home and background	
Appearance	
Actions and behaviour	
Likes and dislikes	
Motives and ambitions	
The reaction of people around him/her • Parents • Teachers	
Abilities and opportunities	

Planning and scaffolding [Criterion 3Diii]

Communicating with a sense of audience

Now think about the language you will use in your text. Choose one of these registers:

• very formal, as if talking politely to a very important stranger
• formal, as if talking very politely to people you don't know well
• informal, as if talking to a friend.

Conclusion to the conceptual question

How difficult is it to achieve our ambitions?

Now that you have looked at Maslow's hierarchy and considered the example of the Cambodian children what is your answer to the question? Are our ambitions limited by our opportunities?

Key and related concepts: Connections and messages

Key concept: Connections

Connections are links, bonds and relationships among people and the society in which they live. This concept is central to the study of language. In Language Acquisition we have to think about the relationships between speaker and audience, writer and reader. We also need to think about the ways messages connect us when we communicate.

Related concept: Message

A message is a communication in writing, speech, verbal or non-verbal language. Messages consist of signals, facts, ideas and symbols. In communication between humans, messages can be verbal (spoken or written), non-verbal (facial expression), visual (image) or a combination of all of these (video). Here are some messages that combine written text and visuals to create their messages.

A message is also the information contained in a communication between a sender and a receiver. Messages contain meaning, as we can see in the example of an email below (visual text 2).

Visual text 1

Visual text 2

Visual text 3

A message can contain literal and concrete, abstract and metaphorical meanings.

Messages are also dependent on the context (time and place) in which they are created and on the relationship between the sender and receiver of the message.

Visual text 4

135

Thinking about connections and messages

Criteria: 3Bi, 3Bii

Look at the four graphics above and answer the following questions.

2 **Multiple choice questions**

Choose the correct answer from A, B, C, or D. Write the letter in the answer box provided.

1. Identify the **form** of the message visual texts 1–4
   A. Advert
   B. Sign
   C. Entertainment
   D. Instruction
   E. Storybook

Visual text 1	Visual text 2	Visual text 3	Visual text 4

2. The **purpose** of the message in visual texts 1–4
   A. Narrate
   B. Explain
   C. Instruct
   D. Persuade
   E. Describe

Visual text 1	Visual text 2	Visual text 3	Visual text 4

3. The **author/sender** of visual texts 1–4 is probably:
   A. An advertiser
   B. An instructor
   C. A journalist
   D. A business
   E. A creative artist

Visual text 1	Visual text 2	Visual text 3	Visual text 4

4. The **readers/recipients** of visual texts 1–4 are:
   A. A general audience
   B. An audience with a specific interest
   C. An audience belonging to a specific age range

Visual text 1	Visual text 2	Visual text 3	Visual text 4

5. The **nature** of the message in visual texts 1–4
   A. Literal and concrete
   B. Abstract and metaphorical

Visual text 1	Visual text 2	Visual text 3	Visual text 4

6. The **format** used in visual texts 1–4 is:
   A. mainly visual
   B. a balance of visual and text
   C. mainly text
   D. all text
   E. all visual

Visual text 1	Visual text 2	Visual text 3	Visual text 4

Formative oral and interactive skills: Discussion

What is a discussion?

A group discussion is a conversation about a particular topic. In Language Acquisition, your discussion will have a practical purpose. It could be to answer a question, solve a problem or conflict, create a plan of action, or organize an event.

In a small group everyone has the opportunity to take part in the discussion. No single person should dominate the discussion and a group of two or three generally doesn't need a leader, or chairperson. However, a larger group may find it useful to select one.

Formative interactive skills: Discussion

Criteria: 3Ci, 3Cii, 3Ciii, 3Civ

Study and discuss this film poster.

The purpose of the discussion is to find meanings in the text. A second purpose of the discussion is to come to conclusions you can all agree on.

In small groups discuss these questions. Use your social skills to negotiate answers you can all agree on.

1. What lessons in life does the father want to communicate to his son?
2. What does the image of the father and son communicate?
3. What is the metaphorical meaning of the bright light next to the two characters' hands.
4. Why do you think the word "HAPPYNESS" is spelled incorrectly?
5. What meaning does this misspelled word communicate?
6. What messages about the film do the advertisers wish to communicate to the public?

At the end of the discussion you need to:

1. come to a conclusion and make a decision
2. decide how to present your conclusion
3. share your ideas with the class.

Which of the above visual texts on page 134 do you prefer? Choose two.

Which visual is technically best? Give a reasoned, logical argument to support one choice.

Which visual provokes the strongest reaction? Choose the other visual for its emotional appeal.

In your opinion, which text is the most successful at communicating its message? What criteria will you use for making a decision?

Research the different techniques that visual and graphic artists use to convey a message. Which ones are used in the four visuals?

Which ones are used most effectively?

Formative written skills: Descriptions and blogs

One way of communicating our ideas is to describe people, places and things. We can also describe our ideas. Sometimes we describe the world around using our five senses: sight, sound, smell, taste and touch. We can also describe our emotions when we experience people, ideas and things: "He gets so excited thinking about the future." Sometimes we describe by comparing one thing to another: "He was as big as a door"; "She ran like lightning"; "It was a monster plan."

One specific context for expressing our thoughts on life is through a blog.

Formative writing activity

You find this picture of a school in Cambodia on the Internet and it inspires you to write a blog describing what you can see and your thoughts and reactions. You may want to think about these questions.

- What is the message in the text? Think again about the concepts of abilities and opportunities.

- Do you agree or disagree with the message in the photograph, "Teachers change lives"?

- What will be your message of your blog? What ideas do you want your audience to understand?

ATL Social skills

Every discussion should have a procedure that you can follow:

1. Brainstorm.
2. Test different ideas.
3. Find the ideas everyone can agree on.
4. Come to a conclusion and make a decision.
5. Decide how to present your conclusion.
6. Share your ideas with the class.

Planning and scaffolding: Accuracy and organization

You may find it helpful to copy and complete the table below.

The title of your blog	
Opening How will you get your audience's attention? What is your big idea?	
Main paragraphs Ideas to support your main idea: What are your main 2–4 points?	A. B. C. D.
Ending Final thought/conclusion You blog should be between 200 and 250 words in length.	

Planning and scaffolding

Think about your audience. Your target audience will be people who share your interests or ideas. When you write your blog, you can address your audience directly. And you can ask your readers to respond to your ideas. You can be quite chatty in your use of language but do not be too informal.

How can we make a difference and help others?

Conceptual question

Before you read Text C

Criteria 3Bi, 3Bii, 3Biii

Focusing questions

What are the messages contained in this picture:

- about the girl/mother?
- about the society in which she lives?

What messages is the text giving to the readers/viewers? Again, think about the concepts of abilities and opportunities.

While reading Text C

Criterion 3Bi

Text C is taken from a website which is looking to make a difference to education. It suggests ways we can help people with fewer opportunities than ourselves to develop their abilities to their maximum potential.

As you read the text, complete these sentences using your own words. Make sure the sentences make grammatical sense.

1. When you feed children, you make it (…1…) for them to go to school.
2. Children who get an education are able to earn (…2…) money as adults.
3. When a girl goes to school, she can (…3…) herself and her family for years to come.
4. An educated farmer knows how to make (…4…) of new farming methods.
5. Poor teaching leads to low (…5…) to stay in school and many children drop out.
6. We can make a difference by making a (…6…) of money for their education.

ATL Social and communication skills

Complete the exercise on the left in pairs.

- First discuss the missing word. Is it a verb, adjective, noun, and so forth.
- Then decide on the best word to fit the gap.
- Use your social skills to make sure that you work together with your partner to find answers that you can both agree on.

Text C

Making a difference

Education quite simply creates sustainable change for children, for families, for communities – for entire countries.

Hunger

- Hunger limits a child's ability to concentrate at school.

- A school breakfast or lunch programme allows children to attend school.

- When you feed children, you make it possible for them to learn.

When children learn, they later earn!

- Children who go to school are able to earn more money as adults.

- One year of primary school increases wages by five to fifteen per cent.

- For each additional year of secondary school, an individual's wages can increase by 15 to 25 per cent.

Educated women have healthy babies

- A child born to a literate mother is 50 per cent more likely to survive past the age of five.

- Educated women can help to support their own families.

- So, when you make it possible for a girl to learn, you make it possible for her to feed herself and her family for years to come.

Education is perhaps the most effective strategy to tackle a country's poverty

- When 40 per cent of adults are able to read and write, a country's economy grows.

- Education allows farmers to make use of new farming techniques and technologies.

Barriers to good education in impoverished nations

- Poor quality education leads to low motivation to stay in school and many children drop out.

- So even when children do attend school, they often struggle to learn in large class sizes.

- They often have untrained and poorly paid teachers using outdated learning materials.

- In sub-Saharan Africa, one in three children who start school does not complete even basic primary school, let alone progress to secondary school.

Child sponsorship and making a gift of money are just two ways to help. Your donations can give children, women and entire communities the gift of education and the tools all people need to reach their full potential.

Adapted from http://www. canadianfeedthechildren.ca/news-views/features/ breaking-the-cycle-of-poverty-with-education

Text handling: Text C

Criteria 3Bi, 3Bii, 3Biii

1 True/false with justification

In this exercise you must reread the text carefully and identify true and false statements. The sentences below are either true or false. Justify each answer with a relevant brief quotation from the text. Write your answers on a separate sheet of paper. Both a correct identification and a quotation are required for one mark.

		True	False
Example:	Hungry children do well at school.		✔
Justification	"Hunger limits a child's ability to concentrate at school."		
1	Educated adults earn the same as the uneducated.		
Justification:			
2	An extra year of education can give an adult 25% more in wages.		
Justification:			
3	A baby is more likely to grow up healthy if the mother has been to school.		
Justification:			
4	An educated girl can make a big positive difference to her family.		
Justification:			
5	Literacy and economic growth are unconnected.		
Justification:			
6	Children learn well in big classes.		
Justification:			

2 Multiple-choice question

One of these statements is false. Choose the incorrect sentence from A, B, C, or D.

7. When there is little money for education:
  A. the teachers get little training
  B. the teachers can earn very little
  C. the teaching is always very poor
  D. the teaching can be very old-fashioned.

3 Short-answer questions

Answer the following questions.

8. The last paragraph suggests two ways we can help. What are they?

9. Which phrase in the final paragraph describes the purpose of education?

4 Research question

10. Do you think Text C is relevant to the education system in your country? Give reasons for your answers.

141

Formative oral and interactive skills: Discussion

Look at the diagram below. It describes a cycle of poverty.

Imagine you are working for a development agency. In pairs discuss and plan a poster about children needing better access to education in your country. Here are some other points to discuss.

- What will be the main message of your poster?

- Who will be the audience for the message?

- How will the audience affect the message?

- What will be the headline? Think about the two related concepts of opportunities and abilities.

- How will you use the visual text below? What pictures will you use to illustrate the message?

- What will be your written text?

- What other visual information will you use to help communicate the overall message of your poster?

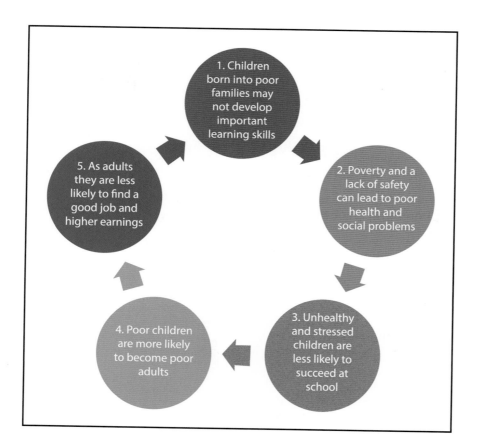

> **ATL Communication and social skills**
>
> In this exercise you have the opportunity to create and communicate messages and information effectively through teamwork.
>
> - Use modes of non-verbal communication effectively.
>
> - Use intercultural understanding to present ideas.
>
> - Use a variety of visual techniques to communicate.
>
> - Use appropriate forms of visual for a specific purpose and audience.

Formative writing skills activity: Poster

Criteria 3Di, 3Dii, 3Diii

Create the poster you have discussed in the previous exercise. Make sure it clearly communicates its message about supporting children who need better access to education in your country. Your poster should contain between 200 and 250 words of written text as well as visual information.

Planning and scaffolding

Criterion 3Diii

Communicating with a sense of audience

Now think about the language you will use to address your audience. First decide whom the poster is aimed at. Then choose one of these registers:

- very formal, as if talking politely to a very important stranger
- formal, as if talking very politely to people you don't know well
- informal, as if talking to a friend.

Conclusion to the conceptual question

How can we make a difference and help others?

Having examined this section, what is your answer to the question? Make a list of practical things we can do to help others with fewer opportunities than ourselves.

Lending a helping hand

ATL Self-management skills

Mindfulness is thinking about yourself in a positive manner. In this book you have many opportunities to reflect on the skills you are developing.

Make a list of the different skills you possess.

Use these headings:

Social skills

Communication skills

Research skills

Thinking skills

(Self-) Management skills

Reflect on how you can use your skills to help others.

How does audio-visual Text D communicate the theme of personal development?

Conceptual question

What do we know so far?

In this chapter you have looked into the topic of abilities and opportunities. As a class, make a list of the most important ideas you have learned so far in your investigations.

At this stage, are there any points you don't understand?

Make a list of your questions.

How many answers can you find in this audio-visual section?

Suggested texts for this section

A. http://www.acesconnection.com/blog/ted-podcast-on-maslow-s-hierarchy-of-needs

Podcast on Maslow's hierarchy of needs

B. https://www.youtube.com/watch?v=QKQ2I73GBK8

Lecture on differences between working class and middle class opportunities

C. https://www.youtube.com/watch?v=iwE1iXf_3ao

The Epic Journey of NFL's Michael Oher

Note: Alternatively, you could use an audio-visual stimulus related to the theme of your own choosing.

Before you watch Text D
Focusing activity
Read through the exercises below to make sure you know what to look and listen for. You may need to watch the materials several times and discuss possible answers in class after each viewing and listening.

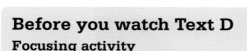 **Research skills**

Media Literacy

In this section you can develop these valuable 21st century learning skills.

- Interacting with media to use and create ideas and information.

- Making informed choices about personal viewing experiences.

- Understanding the impact of media representations.

- Seeking a range of perspectives from varied sources.

- Communicating information and ideas effectively.

While you watch Text D

Criterion 3Ai

Respond to the tasks and answer the questions in the appropriate manner. Write your answers on a separate sheet of paper.

1. This audio-visual stimulus seems to be related to which of these MYP global contexts?
   A. Identities and relationships
   B. Orientation in space and time
   C. Personal and cultural expression
   D. Scientific and technical innovation
   E. Globalization and sustainability
   F. Fairness and development

2. Use the table below to summarize the main points of the stimulus. You may wish to add extra supporting points, if necessary.

	Main idea	Examples and/or explanations and/or details
Subject matter		
Thesis – main point		
Supporting point 1		
Supporting point 2		
Supporting point 3		
Supporting point 4		
Conclusions		

1 **Multiple-choice questions with justifications**

3. The approach to the subject matter of the audio-visual stimulus is mainly:

   A. entertaining
   B. factual
   C. persuasive
   D. other.
   Justification/reason:

4. How would you describe the content of the stimulus?

   Criterion 3Aii

   A. Really interesting
   B. Interesting
   C. Fairly interesting
   D. Uninteresting
   Justification/reason:

2 **Multiple-choice questions**

5. What was the format of the audio-visual stimulus?

   A. Speech
   B. Conversation/discussion
   C. Debate
   D. Documentary
   E. Other ⬜

6. The purpose of the audio-visual stimulus was to:

   A. narrate a story
   B. describe a situation
   C. explain a problem
   D. argue a point of view
   E. give instructions/guidelines
   F. other. ⬜

7. How many points of view did the audio-visual stimulus show?

   A. One
   B. Two
   C. Three
   D. More than three ⬜

8. The opinions in the audio-visual stimulus are:

   A. very balanced
   B. quite balanced
   C. biased
   D. very one-sided. ⬜

9. How much did the audio-visual stimulus use graphics?

   A. A lot
   B. More than twice
   C. Once or twice
   D. Never ⬜

10. Which of these techniques are used in the audio-visual stimulus?

   A. Voiceover
   B. Special lighting techniques
   C. Music and sound effects
   D. Other special effects
   E. None of the above
   F. All of the above
   G. Some of the above ⬜

Formative interactive oral skills: Role-play

In pairs find out what the video has to say about "abilities" and "opportunities".

- Together discuss your understanding of the two concepts.

- Define each concept. List the characteristics of each.

- Discuss the message of the video.

- What examples of "abilities" and "opportunities" does the video give?

- What does the video say about the relationship between "abilities" and "opportunities"?

- Organize your findings and present them to your class.

Formative writing skills: Blog entry

Write up your reactions to the audio-video stimulus you have watched in the form of a blog.

You could mention:

- the reason for watching the audio-visual

- the theme, main points and conclusion

- the extent to which the stimulus interested you

- the extent to which you agree with ideas represented in the stimulus

- the most important conventions and techniques used to make the video.

Use your answers from previous sections to help you plan your blog entry. The best answers will also give examples and justifications.

> **Planning and scaffolding**
>
>
> **Communicating with a sense of audience**
>
> Now think about the language you will use in the blog.

Conclusion to the conceptual question

How does audio-visual Text D communicate the theme of personal development?

Having examined this section, what is your answer to the question?

ATL Research and self-management skills

Have you found answers to all the questions you asked at the beginning of this section? If not, where, and how, do you think you could find the information you are seeking?

Summative activities

In this summative assessment you will have an opportunity to show your understanding of the topics of opportunities, abilities and ambitions. You will also be assessed on your use of the communication skills you have developed in this chapter. To complete the assessment you will undertake two tasks. Each task requires you to answer a debatable question.

Statement of inquiry

We can use language to describe and realize our personal ambitions and abilities and, having done so, define ways in which we can use our abilities to help others.

Debatable question 1

Can service learning help you to develop your own skills and enable you to help others?

Debatable question 2

Do we have to make the most of our opportunities before we can make the most of our abilities?

To answer the first question, you will have to watch a video on service learning and discuss the content. For the second task you will read a single text about refugees to Europe and give your thoughts on the topic.

Summative oral task: Discussion

You have had opportunities to practise discussion skills on a given topic throughout this unit. Now use those skills to answer the following question.

Debatable question 1: Can service learning help you to develop your own skills and enable you to help others?

Assessment task

Watch the following Edutopia video about the value of service learning entitled "Service learning: real-life applications for learning".

http://www.edutopia.org/practice/service-learning-real-life-applications-learning

In small groups make notes on the benefits of service learning from the words and images in the video.

Make sure your discussion comes to an agreed conclusion that answers the debatable question. The discussion should last about 10 to 12 minutes so each person should speak for 3 to 4 minutes.

Alternatively, watch a video on the subject of community service of your own choosing. Make notes on it and conduct a similar discussion.

Text E

Service learning: real-life applications for learning

http://www.edutopia.org/
practice/service-learning-real-life-
applications-learning

You have had opportunities to practise discussions throughout this unit. In this summative assessment you will have a final opportunity to show your understanding of the following learning objectives:

A: Comprehending spoken and visual text

| 3Ai | *Show understanding of information, main ideas and supporting details, and draw conclusions* |

| 3Aii | *Understand conventions* |

| 3Aiii | *Engage with the spoken and visual text by identifying ideas, opinions and attitudes and by making a response to the text based on personal experiences and opinions* |

C: Communicating in response to spoken and/or written and/or visual text

| 3Ci | *Respond appropriately to spoken and/or written and/or visual text* |

| 3Cii | *Interact in rehearsed and unrehearsed exchanges* |

| 3Ciii | *Express ideas and feelings, and communicate information in familiar and some unfamiliar situations* |

| 3Civ | *Communicate with a sense of audience and purpose* |

D: Using language in spoken and/or written form

| 3Di | *Write and/or speak using a range of vocabulary, grammatical structures and conventions; when speaking, use clear pronunciation and intonation* |

| 3Dii | *Organize information and ideas and use a range of basic cohesive devices* |

| 3Diii | *Use language to suit the context* |

Summative written assessment: Thoughts on a topic

You have had a few opportunities to practise writing your thoughts about topics throughout this unit. Now use those skills to answer the following question.

Debatable question 2: Do we have to make the most of our opportunities before we can make the most of our abilities?

Read the following articles and make notes.

Based on the information you read in Text F below, write your thoughts about the debatable question, "Do we have to make the most of our opportunities before we can make the most of our abilities?" Use the story of Liz Murray in Text F to illustrate your ideas about opportunities and abilities. You may choose to write your thoughts in the form of a blog entry, letter to a friend or diary entry.

Write 200–250 words.

You have had opportunities to practise writing your thoughts on a topic throughout this unit. In this summative assessment you will have a final opportunity to show your understanding of the following learning objectives:

B: Comprehending written and visual text

3Bi	*Show understanding of information, main ideas and supporting details, and draw conclusions*
3Bii	*Understand basic conventions including aspects of format and style, and author's purpose for writing*
3Biii	*Engage with the written and visual text by identifying ideas, opinions and attitudes and by making a response to the text based on personal experiences and opinions*

C: Communicating in response to spoken and/or written and/or visual text

3Ci	*Respond appropriately to spoken and/or written and/or visual text*
3Cii	*Interact in rehearsed and unrehearsed exchanges*
3Ciii	*Express ideas and feelings, and communicate information in familiar and some unfamiliar situations*
3Civ	*Communicate with a sense of audience and purpose*

D: Using language in spoken and/or written form

3Di	*Write using a range of vocabulary, grammatical structures and conventions.*
3Dii	*Organize information and ideas and use a range of basic cohesive devices*
3Diii	*Use language to suit the context*

Text F

 www.theguardian.com/world/2010/sep/26/liz-murray-bronx-harvard

Liz Murray: 'My parents were desperate drug addicts. I'm a Harvard graduate'

Joanna Walters

A woman who overcame tremendous odds to go from "homeless to Harvard" has turned her life story into an American bestseller.

Liz Murray, 29, rose from some of New York's meanest streets to graduate from Harvard – an Ivy League university. She has become an international speaker. But some of her earliest memories are of her parents spending their welfare payments on cocaine and heroin when she and her sister were starving: "We ate ice cubes because it felt like eating. We split a tube of toothpaste between us for dinner."

When she became homeless at 16, as well as stealing food she would steal self-help books and study for exams in a friend's hallway. *Now Breaking Night: A Memoir of Forgiveness, Survival, and My Journey from Homeless to Harvard*, has burst on to the *New York Times* bestseller list. Hailed as a "white-knuckle account of survival", it is to be published in Britain in January.

Born in the Bronx, Liz watched her parents mainlining coke all day. "Both my parents were hippies. By the time the early 1980s came around and I'd been born, their disco dancing thing had become a drug habit," she recalls.

She talks frequently about how much she loved them and how much they loved her, how they were highly intelligent but were hopeless at parenting because of their drug dependence and consequent poverty. She remembers her mother stealing her birthday money, selling the television, and even the Thanksgiving turkey a church had given them, to scrape together

Text F *(Continued)*

www.theguardian.com/world/2010/sep/26/liz-murray-bronx-harvard

money to score cocaine. Liz would turn up to school lice-ridden and was bullied for being smelly and scruffy and eventually dropped out.

Her mother's mantra was "one day life is going to be better", then she would spend all day throwing up and being nursed by her daughter or slumped in withdrawal, arms tracked with needle marks. When Liz was 15 her mother revealed that she was HIV-positive and had Aids. She died not long after and was buried in a donated wooden box.

When Liz's father failed to pay the rent on their flat and moved to a homeless shelter, Liz was out on the streets. Her sister got a place on a friend's sofa, but Liz slept on the city's 24-hour underground trains or on park benches.

At first she saw herself as a rebel and a victim, but then she had an epiphany.

"Like my mother, I was always saying, 'I'll fix my life one day.' It became clear when I saw her die without fulfilling her dreams that my time was now or maybe never," she says.

She had nowhere to live and had not attended school regularly for years, but at 17 promised herself to become a "straight A" student and complete her high school education in just two years.

She went to extra night classes and did a year's work each term. A teacher saw her potential and mentored her. When he took his top 10 students to Harvard, Liz stood outside the university and instead of feeling intimidated she admired its architecture – and decided it was within her reach. Then she heard that the *New York Times* gave scholarships.

She was awarded a New York Times scholarship for needy students and was accepted into Harvard University.

Liz is now the founder and director of Manifest Living and a motivational speaker. These days she talks to teenagers about resisting the temptations of drugs and gangs. She also urges them not to use childhood hardship as an excuse not to take opportunities.

Her father died in 2006, also of Aids. His saving grace was that he encouraged her to read – and stole books from libraries to give her a love of literature.

After graduating, she began taking courses at Harvard Summer School with plans to earn a doctorate in clinical psychology and become a counselor.

She doesn't want her appearance now and her Harvard degree to fool anyone: "I was one of those people on the streets you walk away from."

Adapted from https://www.theguardian.com/world/2010/sep/26/liz-murray-bronx-harvard

Going beyond the chapter

In this chapter you have explored the ways in which we can make the most of opportunities, overcome difficulties and achieve our ambitions. You have also looked at ways we can use our skills and talents to make a difference to others. You have learned that we can use language to describe and realize our personal ambitions and abilities and, having done so, define ways in which we can use our abilities to help others. Now make use of the information you have learned and the communication skills you have developed in this chapter for practical purposes beyond the classroom.

Take action! Some suggestions ...

Take control of your future: write your curriculum vitae (CV)

As you go through school, you will start thinking about life beyond the classroom. At this point it is useful to list what skills you have. What are you good at? What are your personal interests? What practical, organizational and personal skills do you possess? What have you achieved so far?

A curriculum vitae, or CV, is a document in which you can present your skills and qualifications in a clear and effective manner. You might need a full CV very soon. You may want to apply to be a volunteer, you might be looking for a holiday job or you may want to apply for a learning opportunity such as a course or an adventure programme. In such cases, you will need to list your skills and achievements.

You might want to talk to your guidance counsellor or homeroom teacher/form tutor for advice on how to go about writing a curriculum vitae.

Discussion

When preparing a CV it is sometimes hard to know what your own skills are. You might not be aware that you can do things that other people may find challenging, such as speak another language or play an instrument.

Look at the chart of "real life skills" above. With your friends, discuss how many of the skills represented in the poster are relevant to teenagers. Use this discussion as a starting point to find out what "real world" skills you each possess.

You could help each other to find out about the things you are each good at. You might even want to discuss these matters with family members or neighbours and family friends who know you well. Use the results of these discussions to help you to write your CV.

Service learning

Speak to your MYP coordinator or action and service coordinator to find out your school's expectations for action and service in your particular grade/year.

The ideas below relate directly to the following service learning outcomes:

- become more aware of your own strengths and areas for growth

- undertake challenges that develop new skills

- discuss, evaluate and plan student-initiated activities

- persevere in action

- work collaboratively with others.

Have another look at the examples of service learning at Montpellier High School described in in Text E.

http://www.edutopia.org/practice/service-learning-real-life-applications-learning

Their projects included developing a school greenhouse, cultivating a garden, and providing food for a lunch programme.

What service learning activity or project could you start and develop, based on your own interests and skills?

Consider the work you did on Maslow's hierarchy of needs (Text B). The investigation section of a service project requires you to think and consider what particular needs a group or community has and how you can use your skills to provide for those needs.

With a group, identify a group of children in your community who require support of one kind or another.

Discuss ways to improve:

A. the basic health needs of the children
B. their safety needs
C. their esteem and educational needs
D. the achievement of their dreams and ambitions.

Formulate an action plan similar to the one you created earlier in this chapter.

If you enjoyed this chapter here are some texts for further reading

Angela N. Blount, *Once Upon a Road Trip*

Elizabeth D. Gray, *I Am Enough: Journal Affirmations for Girls*

Michael Oher, *I Beat the Odds: From Homelessness, to The Blind Side, and Beyond*

Daniel Willey, *Be Great! 365 Inspirational Quotes from the World's Most Influential People*

Jacqueline Woodson, *Brown Girl Dreaming*

ATL Research and thinking skills

At the end of any learning experience always ask yourself these questions:

- What lessons have I learned from this chapter?

- What concepts don't I yet understand about this topic?

- What questions do I still have about this topic?

- Where can I find answers to these questions?

5 Emoticons, emoji and email etiquette

In context

Global context: Scientific and technical innovation

How do we understand the world in which we live?

In this chapter we will explore how we have adapted technology to communicate in new and creative ways.

Key concept

Creativity is the process of creating new ideas and looking at existing ideas from new perspectives. In this chapter we shall look at recent innovations in social media, specifically texting and the use of symbols, such as smiley faces, emoticons and emoji to represent ideas.

Related concept

Conventions are the characteristics of a literary or non-literary genre. Writers use these conventions, along with other features, in order to achieve particular results.

In this chapter we shall look at some of the new informal and formal conventions of texting and writing emails. We will ask whether emoticons and emoji are in fact very creative forms of communication and expression. We shall debate whether these new ways of communicating show that young people are forgetting the conventions needed to express themselves clearly, accurately and formally.

Statement of inquiry

There are social and formal conventions we should use when we communicate but we can still be creative in our use of language, especially in our use of social media.

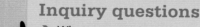

Inquiry questions

→ What are emoticons?

→ What are emoji? How can we use emoji and emoticons both appropriately and creatively?

→ Why do we need rules and etiquette when sending emails?

→ How does audio-visual Text D communicate the theme of emoticons, emoji and email?

→ Can communication take place if we do not have conventions for speaking or writing?

→ Will technological developments soon make formal written language unnecessary?

What are emoticons?

Before you read Text A

Criteria 3Bi, 3Bii

Discussion

What do you know about emiticons and emojis? Before you begin this chapter, conduct a class brainstorming session. You could start by asking, "When is it OK to use emoticons and emojis and when is not OK to use them?"

When we communicate with people face to face, we use facial expressions and a tone of voice. When we write to someone, it is much harder to express the right tone of voice.

An **emoticon** is a set of ordinary keyboard characters. We can use them online to represent a human face. They are used to **convey different emotions**.

Here are some early examples.

Shortcut	Emoji
</3	Broken heart
<3	Purple heart
:D	Grinning face
^_^	Grinning face with smiling eyes
:-) =)	Smiling face with open mouth
=D	Smiling face with open mouth and smiling eyes
O:)	Smiling face with halo
}:)	Smiling face with horns
;)	Winking Face
:|	Neutral face
:\	Confused face
:*	Kissing face
;*	Face throwing a kiss
:P	Face with stuck-out tongue
D:	Frowning face with open mouth
:X)	Grinning cat face with smiling eyes

Look at the emoticons above.

- Which of the emoticons do you use a lot?
- Which of the emoticons do you never use?
- With whom, or in which situations, do you use emoticons when you communicate?

While you read Text A

Criterion 4Bi

In lines 1–10 which words go in the gaps (-x-   ) in the text?
Choose the missing words from the list below.

between	communication	statements
combination	express	through
common	normally	unusual

Text A

Emoticons

The word *emoticon* is a combination of the words *emotion* and *icon*.

They can be made by typing punctuation marks and letters to makes faces in a text.

People use emoticons to (-1-   ) their feelings online, especially when they think that the reader might not understand the message we are sending.

The most (-2-   ) emoticon is a smiley face :)

We can put a dash (-3-   ) the eyes and mouth to make a nose. :-)

This emoticon is (-4-   ) used to convey happiness or a joke. It says to the reader, "This message is not so serious." Let's see what the difference an emoticon can make. Look at the photograph of James receiving a text message from his best friend. Then look at the following two (-5-   ):

A. Idiot

or...

B. Idiot :)

For example, if you were joking with someone and send a text message of "Idiot!" the person receiving your message may think you are making a rude comment to them. If you send the same message with a "happy smiley", the person would then understand you were "smiling" or joking when you said that, and not misinterpret your meaning.

Therefore, without the emoticon James could easily think the first statement (A) is an insult. The second statement (B), however, with its smiling face is very clearly playful and James is not likely to be hurt or offended.

Emoticons can play an important and creative part in online communication. Emoticons with their facial expressions are like the expression in our voices when we speak to someone face to face. Emoticons have become part of the international language of the Internet.

The vast majority of people online have never actually met so they do not know each other well. In such cases it is all too easy to be misunderstood. Emoticons can make online communication easier.

Adapted from: **http://www.wisegeek.com/what-are-emoticons.htm#**

Text handling: factual content of Text A

Criterion 4Bi

1 **Short-answer questions**

Answer the following questions.

6. Why might the best friend's message without a smiley face (A) be unclear to James?

7. How does the emoticon :) make message B clearer to James?

2 **Multiple-choice questions**

Choose the correct answer from A, B, C, or D.

8. Most people talking on the Internet:
   - **A.** are good friends
   - **B.** have met in person
   - **C.** speak the same language
   - **D.** are strangers to each other.

9. In conclusion the writer thinks emoticons are:
   - **A.** poor communication
   - **B.** new and funny
   - **C.** facial expressions
   - **D.** original and influential.

10. The writer also thinks emoticons are like using:
   - **A.** a dictionary
   - **B.** a tone of voice
   - **C.** our emotions
   - **D.** good pronunciation.

Formative oral and interactive skills: Making a presentation

Criteria 3Ci, 3Cii, 3Ciii

In Phase 3 you are expected to speak for 3–4 minutes on a given subject or topic. In the following oral presentation you will practise the skills necessary to complete your final oral presentation at the end of this unit.

The task

You need to give a presentation to a group of young children. The title is "Using emoticons". Using PowerPoint, Prezi, Keynote or a similar presentation program, create a set of slides to present your message. Make sure your message is clear.

Planning and scaffolding

Organizing a presentation

Here are 12 headings. Use the chart to help you decide:

- how many of these headings you would use
- in what order you would put the chosen headings.

Subject of each slide	Use: Yes?/No?	Order
Closing the presentation		
Opening the presentation		
How emoticons communicate the writer's tone of voice		
How to draw emoticons		
Other examples of emoticons		
The most famous emoticon		
The reason for presenting the topic		
What are emoticons?		
What is a tone of voice?		
Where does the word "emoticon" come from?		
Why use emoticons?		
Why writing is different to speaking		

ATL Social skills

Work in pairs or small groups

Here are some useful social skills you can develop during this exercise.

- Building consensus
- Sharing responsibility for planning and decision-making
- Listening actively to other perspectives and ideas
- Encouraging everyone to contribute
- Helping your partner to succeed

Planning and scaffolding   Criterion 3Civ

Communicating with a sense of audience

Now think about the language you will use in the presentation. Think about your audience. Choose one of these registers.

- very formal, as if talking politely to a very important stranger
- formal, as if talking very politely to people you don't know well
- informal, as if talking to a friend.

Formative writing activity: Written advice

Your friend, Michael, really likes Ashley. They've been in the same class for over a year. He's been keeping his feelings to himself, but he would like to invite her out.

He is thinking of sending her a simple text message with an emoticon:

Come to the cinema with me on Saturday ;-)? Michael

Before sending his message he asks you, as a good friend, to ask what you think.

Do you think this message and emoticon are a good idea? How do you think Ashley will react? Could he be more creative?

Using ideas and information from this section send Michael an email with some advice on the matter. You can use emoticons or other symbols. You should aim to write between 200 and 250 words.

Ashley's response

Conclusion to the factual question

What are emoticons?

Having examined this section, what is your answer to the question?

ATL Self-management skills

Before you answer the concluding question, think about what facts you have learned so far.

Consider these three questions:

- What did I learn about in this section?

- What don't I yet understand?

- What questions about this topic do I have now?

What are emoji? How can we use emoji and emoticons both appropriately and creatively?

Conceptual question

Before you read the Text B

Criteria 3Bi, 3Bii

Discussion

You may have noticed that when you're chatting online, your simple emoticon is often automatically converted into a yellow

smiley. These smileys and other symbols are called emoji.

What are the similarities and differences between emoji and emoticons?

Is there is any difference between the smileys that look like this :) and smileys that look like this 😊? You may want to think about appearance, use and any other differences you can think of. Copy and complete the table below.

Similarities	Emoticons and emoji	Differences
	Appearance	
	Use	
	Other points	

ATL Research and communication skills

In this section you will find an number of research questions.

How can you find answers to these questions?

A) Interact with media to use and create ideas and information.

- Locate information from a variety of digital sources.
- Conduct an Internet search.

B) Communicate ideas effectively through interaction.

- Present your findings with the rest of your class.
- Choose an appropriate medium to communicate your findings.

ATL Research and communication skills

Research question one

While the technology is fun and creative, we need to also ask ourselves, "Is it appropriate to use emoticons and emoji?" Are there situations in which it is inappropriate to use them?

http://www.webopedia.com/ TERM/S/smiley.html

Smileys and emoji

Smileys

Smileys are often used in text communications to put an emotion into our messages. Smileys are used in text messages in the same way we use the tone of our voice in face-to-face conversations.

To create a smiley you can use letters and punctuation marks. Frequently the software you are using can convert the characters into a face. Alternatively you can add smileys from a menu. Smileys are often used in online chat rooms, game rooms, instant messaging, and email.

Emoji

Shigetaka Kurita created the first emoji in 1998 or 1999 in Japan. Kurita took inspiration from weather forecast symbols and from manga comics. He created 180 symbols to express emotions and ideas. One such symbol was a light bulb that meant "a great idea".

In 1997 Nicolas Loufrani started experimenting with animated smiley faces. He wanted to create colourful icons that corresponded to existing emoticons made of punctuation marks.

He then created an online dictionary that had different categories of emoji such as Moods, Celebrations, Fun, Sports, Weather, Animals, Food, Nations, Occupations, Planets, Zodiac, and Babies.

In 2000 the Loufrani's Directory was made available for cell phone users on the internet through smileydictionary.com which compiled over 1000 smiley graphics. The rest is history.

Today emoji have become an unofficial universal language in online communication. To older generations it seems that many teenagers are born knowing the meaning of each symbol. Some say emoji have helped create a new way of communicating.

However, as more people and different cultures use emoji, so their meanings can change too depending on the culture and context in which the emoji are used.

In many cases, the original emoji were based on Japanese culture. But people have since adopted entirely new uses and meanings for certain symbols. For example, here are some emoji created for Nigeria. Adapted from: http://www.webopedia.com/ TERM/S/smiley.html

ATL Research and thinking skills

Research question two

Answer the following question.

In your opinion why have they introduced specific emoji in Nigeria?

Text handling: Factual assessment of Text B

Criteria 3Bi, 3Bii

1 True/false with justification

In this exercise you must read the text carefully and identify true and false statements.

Copy the table below. The sentences it contains are either true or false. Tick [✔] the correct response. Justify your answer with information from the poster.

Both a tick and a quotation are required for one mark.

		True	False
Example:	Smileys can help to express our feelings when we text.	✔	
Justification:	Smileys are often used in text communications to put emotions into our messages.		

		True	False
1.	You only need letters to create smileys.		
Justification:			
2.	Smileys are used with many different kinds of software.		
Justification:			
3.	Some of the first emojis came from symbols found in Japanese comics.		
Justification:			
4.	Nicholas Loufrani wanted to make emoticons more interesting to look at.		
Justification:			
5.	Loufrani's dictionary was published as a book.		
Justification:			
6.	Today emojis are used by both young and old.		
Justification:			

2 Multiple-choice question

Choose the correct answer from A, B, C, or D.

7. What do these changes in meaning tell us about the relationship between language and culture?
   A. Languages and symbols are the same in all cultures.
   B. All languages use the same symbols.
   C. No two cultures use the same symbols.
   D. Different cultures can adapt symbols from another culture.

ATL Research and thinking skills

Research question three

Look at the Nigerian emoji above on page 163. What do you think the symbols might mean? Hint: You may wish to use other source material before answering.

Formative oral and interactive skills: Presentation

Criteria 3Ci, 3Cii, 3Ciii

Are emoji a creative use of language?

Some teachers say that emoji are ruining language. They say that the use of texting and emoji will destroy young people's ability to use English properly. Soon students will no longer be able to write formally. Others say this is a new and creative way of communicating. What do you think?

In small groups, sort out the statements below into these two opposing traditional and non-traditional arguments. The purpose of the discussion will be to come to an agreement. The discussion should take 10 to 15 minutes, depending on the size of the group.

- are a new kind of language
- are a whole new way of writing
- allow bad spelling
- are developed by young people
- can create messages quickly
- are childish
- are disrespectful to adults
- are energetic
- are fine to use among friends
- are friendlier
- are fun
- are a new way of communicating
- help to find the right meaning
- let you write the way we talk
- make the writer look stupid
- make you forget about capital letters or punctuation
- make you forget to write grammatically
- make you write like you speak
- are necessary to make the message clearer
- are not proper writing at all
- send the wrong message
- show your mood and emotions
- make the reader look stupid
- worsen writing ability

ATL Social skills

Here are some useful social skills you can develop during this group exercise.

- Building consensus
- Sharing responsibility for planning and decision-making
- Listening actively to other perspectives and ideas
- Encouraging everyone to contribute
- Helping all members of the group to succeed
- Give and receive meaningful feedback

Planning and scaffolding

Argument A (traditional view): Because of texting and emoji, young people will soon no longer be able to write properly	Argument B (non-traditional view): Texting and emojis are a very creative way of using language

Once you have finished categorizing the information, make sure your group can justify your ideas. Using the advice given earlier in this chapter, create a 3–4-minute presentation to give to your class. Divide the presentation so that everyone in the group has a chance to speak.

Planning and scaffolding   Criterion 3Civ

Communcating with a sense of audience
Now think about the language you will use in the presentation to your class. Think about your audience. Choose one of these registers:
- very formal, as if talking politely to a very important stranger
- formal, as if talking very politely to people you don't know well
- informal, as if talking to a friend

Formative written activity: Instructions for use

Criteria 3Ci, 3Cii, 3Ciii, 3Civ

You school has decided it needs some clear rules about the use of emoticons and emojis in students' written schoolwork.

Write a set of dos and don'ts for using emoji in communications:

A. with friends,

B. for schoolwork

C. for formal emails such as college applications.

The best answers will give examples and justifications of your instructions. You should aim to write between 200 and 250 words. You may wish to use the chart below to plan your ideas.

Planning and scaffolding

	Dos	Don'ts
Texting with friends		
School work		
Formal emails		

Conclusion to the conceptual question

How can we use emoji and emoticons appropriately and creatively?

Having examined this section, what is your answer to the conceptual question?

Key and related concepts: Creativity and convention

Criteria 3Bi, 3Bii, 3Biii

Creativity

Creativity is the process of generating novel ideas and considering existing ideas from new perspectives. In this chapter we are looking at emoticons and emoji as new creative ways of communicating ideas. Creativity is also developed through the process of learning a language. You are being creative by applying ideas and expressing opinions in English in order to come to conclusions about a topic.

Conventions in writing

Conventions are the characteristics of any text type. These features may, of course, vary between languages. Every form of writing has recognizable rules, and these are known as conventions. For example there are different conventions for writing a recipe for a magazine, an email to a friend, or an essay for a teacher.

We can be **creative** with language, such as when we write poetry or when we use emoji in texting or online gaming. But there are also times when we must use **conventions** in order to communicate effectively and to achieve a particular purpose.

Look at the image below. How do the concepts of creativity and conventions relate to ideas about the functioning of the left and right sides of the brain?

ATL | Thinking skills

Here is an opportunity to use your creative thinking skills

Work in groups of three or four. Study the poster on the human brain at the bottom of this page and think about the question "What does it mean?"

Make a list of the different parts of the poster. Ask yourself a series of questions about their meaning.

What can you say about the meaning of the poster. When you answer your own questions, make guesses, ask yourself "What might that mean?" Be inventive.

When you have finished create a diagram in order to convey your findings. Think about the techniques you can use so that the diagram communicates your ideas clearly and effectively.

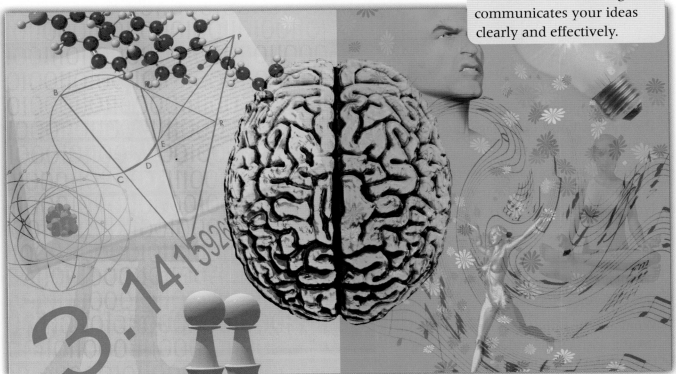

Emoticons, emoji and email etiquette

ATL Research and thinking skills

What do you already know about conventions in writing?

Use brainstorming to generate information.

Next ask: "What don't I know?" and "What don't I yet understand?"

Make a list of questions you have about conventions.

Ask yourself: "Where and how can I find answers to my questions?"

Choose the best place to find answers to your questions.

Let's look at conventions in writing.

To the right is a formal email.

What conventions of email writing can you identify in the text? What other conventions of formal writing can you identify? How do these conventions help the writer to communicate politely? How do these conventions help the writer to communicate the message clearly? What effect will the email have on the reader, Ms Felstead?

Subject: Your visit to (name of school)

Dear Ms Felstead,

I would like to thank you for talking with me during Careers Day at our school on (date). I really appreciate your attention during such a busy event.

As a result of our conversation, I have become very interested in studying (subjects).

At the time you said I could contact you and visit your office and speak to you further. Please inform me if this is possible and when the most convenient time would be.

Thank you again for your time

Sincerely,

(Your name)

ATL Research and thinking skills

It is also important to understand that the conventions of language can change over time.

In the picture you can see hieroglyphics from Ancient Egypt. The text was written about 3,000 years ago.

In what ways has written language changed in these 3,000 years?

To what extent are emoji similar to these hieroglyphics?

What are the differences between texting with emoji and formal writing in English?

Thinking about creativity and conventions

Criteria 3Bi, 3Bii, 3Biii

The questions in this section are designed to test your creativity and imagination.

1. The table below compares formal writing with the use of emojis in text. In groups, think about the conventions surrounding the two different channels of communication according to these four different criteria: spelling, vocabulary, grammar and word order. You may wish to add more criteria to the list.

	Formal writing	Emoji
Spelling		
Vocabulary		
Grammar		
Word order		

2. How will we communicate in the year 2030? Will we still use writing? Will the future be like this?

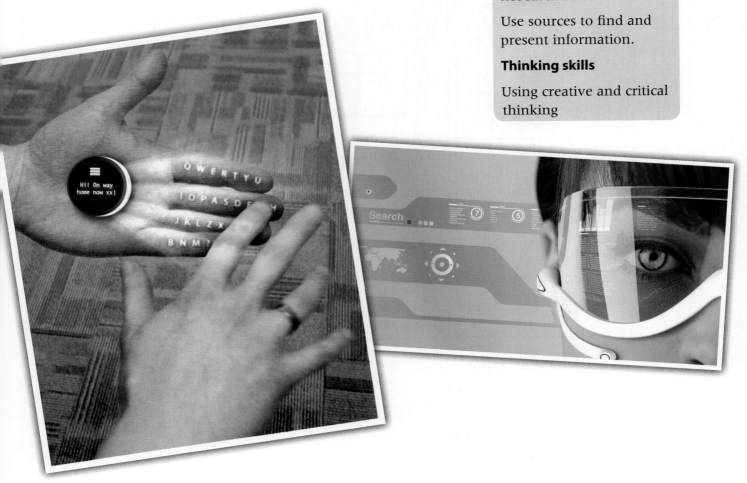

3. Or will the future of writing be unchanged?

   How will we use the new technologies?

   How effective will they be?

THE BOOK OF THE FUTURE

GRANT SNIDER

4. What is the message of this cartoon? Does the cartoonist think that books have a future?

5. How do you think the English language may change in the next 10–15 years?

- Will the conventions of writing remain the same?

- Which conventions will change?

Formative oral and interactive skills

Oral presentation

During the Language Acquisition course you may be asked to give an oral presentation on a topic you have studied. When you present it is very important do the following.

A. Select appropriate material for the presentation.

- How many ideas will you use?

B. Organize your ideas into a clear structure.

- In what order would you put your ideas?

171

Planning and scaffolding

You have to give a short presentation for 3 or 4 minutes to your class on texting. Here are some ideas for the presentation. You may wish to add more ideas.

Subject of each slide	Use? Yes/No
1. Closing the presentation – How?	
2. Opening the presentation – How?	
3. What is texting?	
4. Why do teenagers like texting?	
5. What are emoji and emoticons?	
6. Why use emoji?	
7. Your reason for presenting the topic.	
8. Where do the words emoticon and emoji come from?	
9.	
10.	

You cannot talk about everything, so choose no more than five headings.

Put the five headings in the best order, so that your audience can follow your presentation as easily as possible.

Formative oral activity – presentation

Criteria 3Ci, 3Cii, 3Ciii ,3Civ

In pairs or groups of three, you are going to plan an English class party. Make a list of all the things that need to happen. Then make a list of all the things that the group will have to do to make sure that the party is successful. Present your ideas to your English class using presentation software, such as Prezi or Powerpoint. You may use emoticons and emoji to communicate your ideas.

Before you start your presentation, discuss the differences between good and poor public presenters.

In your time at school you have probably listened to a huge number of speakers. Some presenters communicate well and make you interested in the subject of the talk. Other speakers are so boring that you soon stop listening.

What are the differences between great speakers and poor ones?

Share ideas and make a list and then use a visual diagram to categorize and display your ideas.

Take the lessons you have learned and apply them to your own presentation.

Making a presentation in public can be a very stressful process.

Use the information in this chapter and the skills you have developed to produce a really clear presentation.

Planning and scaffolding

Write all your ideas out on scraps of paper.

Create headings for the main ideas

Shift the pieces of paper around until all the instructions are in the best possible structure.

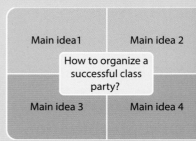

Next, if necessary, arrange the individual points in each main idea into the correct sequence.

Prepare a presentation to the class. Each person should speak between 3 -4 minutes. You may use emojis and emoticons to communicate your ideas. You may wish to record your presentation.

In order to succeed make sure that everyone in the group takes part in the planning and delivery of the speech. That way everyone in the group is working for success.

Each person should speak for 1–2 minutes. You may wish to record your presentation. At the end you can vote on whose ideas are best and whose presentation was the most enjoyable.

Formative writing skills: Instructions, guidelines and advice

Instructions **tell** you what to do or how to act. Guidelines and advice **suggest** what to do. Study the photograph opposite. What instructions might the visiting medical student be giving to the Biology class?

"And this is how to remove a non-essential body part!"

Tone and audience

The relationships between reader and writer can be seen in the way the writer or speaker modifies the instructions. Guidelines and advice can be more personal in style and address, depending on the topic and the relationship between the writer and the audience.

Command: Do it!
Instruction: Do it this way.
Advice: It would be good to do it like this.
Suggestion: I suggest you do it.
Hint: You might wish to do it.

Structure

Instructions, such as recipes, are chronological. They start at the beginning and finish at the end. Therefore they can be represented by a timeline.

Start | Step 1 | 2 | Step 2 | 3 | Step 3 | etc. | End

How to cook my favourite meal

This structure could also be used for other sets of "how to" instructions.

On the other hand you can organize guidelines as if you were offering solutions to a problem.

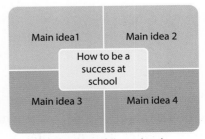

How to be successful at school

Formative assessment: Instructions/guidelines

Criteria 3Di, 3Dii, 3Diii

Write up one or more of these sets of instructions to your fellow students.

1. How to use the conventions of formal writing to influence a reader you need to impress

2. Ten steps to prepare the perfect presentation

3. How to use emoticons and emojis in SMS texting

Before you write, think about the structure of the text you are going to write. Will you:

A. use a linear structure

B. use a structure that offers solutions to a problem?

Make a note of all your ideas before you write and submit your final draft.

As these are semi-formal texts, you can use a limited number of emojis in your text.

For each set of instructions you should aim to write between 200 and 250 words.

Planning and scaffolding

Things to think about when writing a set of instructions:

- Write a title?
- Use headings?
- Use bullet points?
- Use emoji and emoticons?
- Who is the audience?
- Will you use formal, semi-formal or informal language?

Why do we need rules and etiquette when sending emails?

Before you read Text A

Focusing discussion

Look at the cartoon. What is its message about English teaching? Do you think this will be the English class of tomorrow?

Despite the rise in texting and the use of emoticons, there is still a place for formal communications. As we have already seen in this chapter, not all correspondence you will write will be to personal friends or peers on the Internet. We also need to know the conventions about writing to an institution, such as a school, a university or a company.

How many conventions of formal writing do you know? Make a list.

175

While you read Text C

The guidelines in Text C were written for students at an American university.

How many of the conventions of formal writing you listed in the discussion above are mentioned in the text?

Planning and scaffolding

Points to think about:

- Features of an email: sender, recipients, title, body

- Language: formal or informal?

- Opening and closing: how to start and how to finish

- Emoji and emoticons: when to use and not to use

Text C

http://www.it.cornell.edu/services/guides/email/polite.cfm

Email etiquette

To be a good student and to protect yourself and others, follow these guidelines when sending electronic mail.

What to do

Address your messages correctly.

Write your message carefully. Once you send an email message, you cannot take it back or make it disappear.

Use upper and lowercase text properly. Using all uppercase letters means SHOUTING. See what I mean? People may find it very annoying, and harder to read.

Sign your messages with your name.

Use the **To, Cc,** and **Bcc** fields correctly. Here are a couple of simple guidelines:

- When sending to people who know each other, it's okay to put their addresses in the **To:** field.

- When sending to many people who don't know each other, put their addresses in the **Bcc:** field. (Why? Using the Bcc field means you're not sharing them with everyone on the email list.)

You may indicate humor or jokes with a sideways smiley face. :-)

Be calm. Don't reply while you're still angry (this is called "flaming").

Be brief.

Watch out for viruses and other threats in attached files. If you don't know why you got an attachment, contact the sender quickly to find out what the attachment is.

What not to do

Don't forward chain mail or junk mail! These messages often ask you to send or forward them to several other people. Nobody wants them.

Don't forward emails unless you have the permission of the author. Their message may not have been intended for a wider audience, so it's always better to ask.

http://www.it.cornell.edu/services/guides/email/
polite.cfm

Text handling: Factual understanding of Text C

Criteria 3Bi, 3Bii, 3Biii

1 Short-answer questions

Answer the following questions.

1. Why do we need to read a message before sending it?
2. Which word describes the effect of a message sent in uppercase letters?
3. Which two pieces of advice does the writer give for closing an email?

2 Multiple-choice questions

Choose the correct answer from A, B, C, or D.

4. We use the **To:** field when we are sending to:
   A. a few people we know well
   B. a large number of people who don't know each other very well
   C. a large number of people we do know very well
   D. a small number of people who don't know each other.

5. We use the **Bcc:** field when we are sending to:
   A. a few people we know well
   B. a number of people who don't know each other
   C. a large number of people we do know very well
   D. a small number of people who know each other quite well.

6. The phrase "be brief" means be:
   A. little
   B. polite
   C. quick
   D. short.

3 Short-answer questions

7. The writer says it is possible to use a smiley. When?
8. What does the word "flaming" mean?
9. What advice does the writer give about possible viruses?
10. Which phrase explains why you should not forward junk mail or chain mail?
11. Why should you ask permission to forward somebody's email?

In conclusion, why is it important to have rules and conventions when sending emails at college or in other formal situations?

ATL Social and thinking skills

In pairs discuss these two concluding questions:

1 Why is it important to have rules and conventions when sending emails at college or in other formal situations?

2 What conventions should you use when sending emails to your teachers?

Find evidence and justifications for your answers.

Be prepared to discuss your answers in class.

Oral and interactive skills: Presentation

Criteria 3Ci, 3Cii, 3Ciii, 3Civ

You and your friends have created a dog-walking service and have already created an advertisement (see below). Now prepare a presentation for your dog-walking service to go on your website.

Planning and scaffolding

- Present five to ten slides.
- Find a title/subject for each slide.
- Write the content of each slide.
- Use formal but friendly language.
- Be very professional in your presentation.
- Use the correct level of formality.
- Use emoji sparingly.

ANYTOWN DOG WALKER SERVICES

If you do not have time to walk your dogs, I can do it for you.
I am dependable and good with pets, especially dogs, and know how to go about exercising and looking after them.

Contact information

Name: Anne Other

Phone: 0123456789

Email: dogwalkers@internet.com

Website: www.anytowndogwalkers.com

Formative writing activity: Formal email

Criteria 3Di, 3Dii, 3Diii

Your dog-walking service receives the following email.

http://www.it.cornell.edu/services/guides/email/polite.cfm

To: dogwalkers@internet.com

Subject: Your advert

Dear Anne,

I have a two-year-old terrier that needs exercising during the week. I live on Main Avenue.

Please email me with details of yourself and your service.

Thank you

A N Owner

Write a formal but friendly reply. Use between 200 and 250 words.

Planning and scaffolding

Things to think about:

- Features of an email: sender, recipients, title, body
- Language: formal or informal?
- Opening and closing: how to start and how to finish?
- Use of emojis and emoticons: to use or not to use?
- What information will you use to convince your client that you can provide a suitable service?

Conclusion to the conceptual question

Why do we need rules and etiquette when sending emails?

Having examined this section, what is your answer to the question? Do we really need rules or are they simply a waste of time or a restriction on our freedom to express ourselves?

How does audio-visual Text D communicate the theme of emoticons, emoji and email?

Conceptual question

Before you watch Text D

What do we know so far?

In this chapter you have looked into the topic of etiquette in communication. As a class, make a list of the most important ideas you have learned so far in your investigations.

At this stage, are there any points you don't understand?

Make a list of your questions.

How many answers can you find in this audio-visual section?

Suggested texts for this section

A. https://www.youtube.com/watch?v=J6-CnO0kuu4

Emoji: The Future Of Language?

B. https://www.youtube.com/watch?v=Bd3ON8nq4v0

Emoji is the World's Newest Language

C. https://www.youtube.com/watch?list=PLxRhTjvLlyoJpqRIGDb7Ab8qWVLy6JN1x&v=IbHBVS2IDro

Bill Nye Explains How You Dream with Emoji

D. https://www.youtube.com/watch?v=8tWZ2JmFpx0

Are Emoticons the Future of Language?

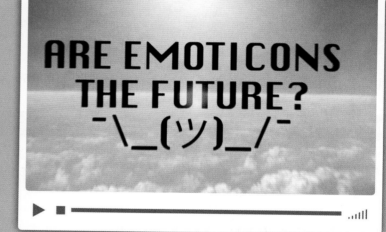

Note: Alternatively, you could use an audio-visual stimulus related to the theme of emoticons, emoji and email of your own choosing.

Before you watch Text D

Focusing activity

Read through the exercises below to make sure you know what to look and listen for. You may need to watch the materials several times and discuss possible answers in class after each viewing and listening.

While you watch Text D

Respond to the tasks and answer the questions in the appropriate manner.

1. This audio-visual stimulus seems to be related to which of these MYP global contexts?

   A. Identities and relationships

   B. Orientation in space and time

   C. Personal and cultural expression

   D. Scientific and technical innovation

   E. Globalization and sustainability

   F. Fairness and development

2. Copy this table and use it to summarize the main points of the stimulus. You may wish to add extra supporting points, if necessary.

	Main idea	Examples and/or explanations and/or details
Subject matter		
Thesis – main point		
Supporting point 1		
Supporting point 2		
Supporting point 3		
Supporting point 4		
Conclusions		

1 Multiple-choice questions with justifications and evidence

1. The approach to the subject matter of the audio-visual stimulus is mainly:

   A. entertaining

   B. factual

   C. persuasive

   D. other:

   Justification/reason:

   Evidence from audio-visual text:

2. How would you describe the content of the stimulus?

   A. Really interesting

   B. Interesting

   C. Fairly interesting

   D. Uninteresting

   Justification/reason:

   Evidence from audio-visual text:

ATL Research skills

Media Literacy

In this section you can develop these valuable 21st century learning skills.

- Interacting with media to use and create ideas and information.

- Making informed choices about personal viewing experiences.

- Understanding the impact of media representations.

- Seeking a range of perspectives from varied sources.

- Communicating information and ideas effectively.

181

2 **Multiple-choice questions**   Criterion 3Aii

Answer the following questions 5–10.

3. What was the format of the audio-visual stimulus?
    A. Speech
    B. Conversation/discussion
    C. Debate
    D. Documentary
    E. Other   ☐

4. The purpose of the audio-visual stimulus was to:
    A. narrate a story
    B. describe a situation
    C. explain a problem
    D. argue a point of view
    E. give instructions/guidelines.
    F. Other: ☐

5. How many points of view did the audio-visual
    stimulus show?
    A. One
    B. Two
    C. Three
    D. More than three   ☐

6. The opinions in the audio-visual stimulus are:
    A. very balanced
    B. quite balanced
    C. biased
    D. very one-sided.   ☐
    Justification:

7. How much did the audio-visual stimulus
    use graphics?
    A. A lot
    B. More than twice
    C. Once or twice
    D. Never   ☐

8. Which of these techniques are used in the
    audio-visual stimulus?
    A. Voiceover
    B. Special lighting techniques
    C. Music and sound effects
    D. Other special effects
    E. None of the above
    F. All of the above
    G. Some of the above   ☐

Formative interactive oral: Presentation

Criterion 3Aiii

The purpose of this presentation is to summarize ideas and techniques used in the audio-visual stimulus to another class who have not seen it.

Working in groups, use the information in your answers to questions 1 to 8 to construct a presentation on the content and the techniques used. Your presentation should be 3–4 minutes long.

Planning and scaffolding
Criteria 3Civ, 3Di

Before you give an individual presentation you should work in groups to discuss ideas and then refine them.

- What are the main points from the video you want to communicate?
- Discuss the headings you could use for your points.
- Discuss the order of those headings.
- Make notes on each heading.
- Find visuals that will help you to communicate your ideas.
- Divide up the presentation and practise your parts individually and then put them together.
- Pay attention to vocabulary, grammatical structures and conventions.
- Remember to use clear pronunciation and intonation.

Planning and scaffolding
Criterion 3Civ

Communicating with a sense of audience

Now think about the language you will use in the presentation. Think about your audience. Choose one of these registers:

- very formal, as if talking politely to a very important stranger
- formal, as if talking very politely to people you don't know well
- informal, as if talking to a friend.

ATL Communication skills

In this activity you can practice using communication skills to produce a clear and effective presentation. There are a number of things that you can do.

- Use verbal communication effectively.
- Use a variety of speaking techniques to communicate with an audience.
- Use appropriate forms of note-taking.
- Use a variety of media platforms to communicate with a range of audiences.
- Negotiate ideas and knowledge with your group and your teacher.
- Participate in, and contribute to, group activities.
- Collaborate with your group to create a digital media product.
- Share your ideas using a variety of print and digital media.

Formative writing activity: Instructions, guidelines and advice

Having watched the video and analysed the content, what lessons have you learned about language, communication and the use of technology?

Make a list of any or all of the points mentioned in the audio-visual stimulus you have watched.

Planning and scaffolding

You may want to watch the video again to gather ideas. You can copy and use this chart to collect ideas.

	Lessons we have learned from the video
How we communicate	
How we create meaning	
How technology is changing the way we communicate	
Why we need rules when we communicate	
Grammar and language rules	
How we can be creative when we communicate	
Emoticons	
Emoji	
Email etiquette	

Using this information, write a set of guidelines or instructions for younger MYP students. The title is "Some tips on being a successful 21st century communicator". You should aim to write between 200 and 250 words.

Planning and scaffolding · Criterion 3Diii

Communicating with a sense of audience

Now think about the language you will use in the presentation. Think about your audience. Choose one of these registers:

- very formal, as if talking politely to a very important stranger
- formal, as if talking very politely to people you don't know well
- informal, as if talking to a friend.

Conclusion to the conceptual question

How does audio-visual Text D communicate the theme of emoticons, emoji and email?

Having examined this section, what is your answer to the question?

ATL Research and self-management skills

Have you found answers to all the questions you asked at the beginning of this section? If not, where, and how, do you think you could find the information you are seeking?

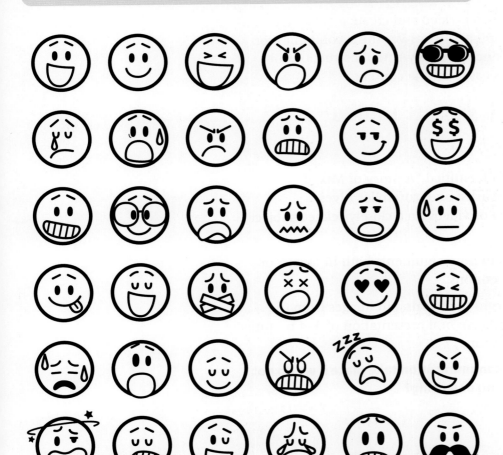

Summative activities

In this summative assessment you will have an opportunity to show your understanding of the topic of emoticons, emojis and email etiquette. You will also be assessed on your use of the communication skills you have developed in this chapter. To complete the assessment you will undertake two tasks related to the statement of inquiry for this chapter. Each assessment task requires you to answer a debatable question.

Statement of inquiry

There are social and formal conventions we should use when we communicate but we can still be creative in our use of language, especially in our use of social media.

Debatable question 1

Can communication take place if we do not have conventions for speaking or writing?

Debatable question 2

Will technological developments soon make formal written language unnecessary?

For the first task you will watch a video and create a presentation of 3–4 minutes based on the content. To answer the second question, you will read a text and produce a set of written instructions or guidelines of 200–250 words based on the content.

Summative assessment task 1: Presentation

Watch the following TED Talk entitled "A Story of Mixed Emoticons" by performance artist and storyteller Rives. Alternatively, watch a video or videos on a closely related subject of your own choosing.

Make notes. You may wish to note arguments both in favour of and against the use of conventions.

Using evidence/examples from the words and images from the video text(s), create and make an oral presentation of 3–4 minutes' duration to answer the question:

Debatable question 1: Can communication take place if we do not have conventions for speaking or writing?

You have had opportunities to practise oral presentations throughout this unit. In this summative assessment you will have an opportunity to show your understanding of the following learning objectives:

Criterion A: Comprehending spoken and visual text

3Ai *Show understanding of information, main ideas and supporting details, and draw conclusions*

3Aii *Interpret conventions*

3Aiii *Engage with the spoken and visual text by identifying ideas, opinions and attitudes and by making a response to the text based on personal experiences and opinions*

Criterion C: Communicating in response to spoken and/or written and/or visual text

3Ci *Respond appropriately to spoken and/or written and/or visual text*

3Cii *Interact in rehearsed and unrehearsed exchanges*

3Ciii *Express ideas and feelings, and communicate information in familiar and some unfamiliar situations*

3Civ *Communicate with a sense of audience and purpose*

Criterion D: Using language in spoken and/or written form

3Di *Write and/or speak using a range of vocabulary, grammatical structures and conventions; when speaking, use clear pronunciation and intonation*

3Dii *Organize information and ideas and use a range of basic cohesive devices*

3Diii *Use language to suit the context*

Text E

Video: "A story of mixed emoticons"

https://www.ted.com/talks/rives_tells_a_story_of_mixed_emoticons

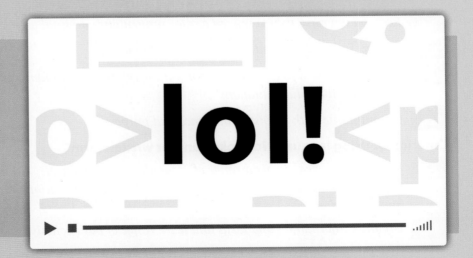

Summative assessment 2: Written guidelines

You have had opportunities to practise writing guidelines and instructions throughout this unit. Now use those skills to answer the following question.

Debatable question 2: Will technological developments soon make formal written language unnecessary?

Read the following article (Text F) and blog post (Text G). Based on the information you read in the two texts, write a set of guidelines for younger students. The guidelines should explain:

A. when the use of emoji and emoticons is acceptable

B. when the use of formal written language is more appropriate.

Write between 200 and 250 words.

You have had opportunities to practise writing guidelines throughout this unit. In this summative assessment you will have a final opportunity to show your understanding of the following learning objectives:

Criterion B: Comprehending written and visual text

3Bi *Show understanding of information, main ideas and supporting details, and draw conclusions*

3Bii *Understand basic conventions including aspects of format and style, and author's purpose for writing*

3Biii *Engage with the written and visual text by identifying ideas, opinions and attitudes and by making a response to the text based on personal experiences and opinions*

Criterion C: Communicating in response to spoken and/or written and/or visual text

3Ci *Respond appropriately to spoken and/or written and/or visual text*

3Cii *Interact in rehearsed and unrehearsed exchanges*

3Ciii *Express ideas and feelings, and communicate information in familiar and some unfamiliar situations*

3Civ *Communicate with a sense of audience and purpose*

Criterion D: Using language in spoken and/or written form

3Di *Write and/or speak using a range of vocabulary, grammatical structures and conventions; when speaking, use clear pronunciation and intonation*

3Dii *Organize information and ideas and use a range of basic cohesive devices*

3Diii *Use language to suit the context*

http://www.cnbc.com/2015/06/24/emojis-the-death-of-the-written-language.html

Emoji: The death of the written language?

Emoji – a Japanese term which translates to "picture and character" – first surfaced in 1998. But it wasn't until smartphones integrated emoji into their operating system that their use took off.

The emergence of these new pictures has added personality to our text message conversations.

"Emoji … are so useful for enriching text with the kinds of things we might convey with our tone of voice or facial expressions," said Tyler Schnoebelen, who has a PhD in linguistics from Stanford.

Tech enthusiast and CEO of Hotel Tonight, Sam Shank, says: "Emoji became popular because as people on mobiles write shorter and shorter messages to each other, it is hard to convey exact meaning.

"For example, does saying that something is 'interesting' mean that it is 'very cool' or 'really lame'? This is actually much easier to convey using emoji," he added.

Emoji were first used in addition to a written text. But now you're finding that a larger group of tech-savvy individuals are replacing words with cartoon symbols to convey a message.

This should be ringing alarm bells. My worry is that we increasingly rely on different smileys or hand gestures to communicate a feeling or expression.

"The person you're sending them to may not know the meaning of an emoji - or misinterpret it," said Hotel Tonight's Shank.

The tone of someone's voice is lost when a text message is used to converse, resulting in the recipient not always understanding the full meaning. For instance, if you are in a new relationship and you fail to recognize what your potential partner is trying to say, this can lead to big problems.

And you don't need to be a psychologist to understand what happens next.

Ben Zimmer, executive editor of Vocabulary.com, says it's the emoji's ambiguous meaning that could lead to confusion because users can look at an emoji and understand different things from it. In addition the use of emojis changes depending on the context and culture.

Here's one example Zimmer provided: the emoji that illustrates two folded hands. According to Zimmer, this emoji started in Japan where the symbol represented salutation or gratitude. Other cultures interpret this emoji to symbolize prayer, while Westerners often see this symbol belonging to two different people giving each other a high five.

Language and communication classes teach students how to use words to tell a story and communicate effectively. If these classes need to incorporate the language and symbols used in the mobile/digital world, aren't we just going back to the age of hieroglyphs?

Adapted from "Emojis: The Death of the Written Language" by Seema Mody

http://www.cnbc.com/2015/06/24/emojis-the-death-of-the-written-language.html

Text G

No, the rise of the emoji doesn't spell the end of language

The emoji has become one of the fastest growing forms of communication in history. People worry about the death of written language. But they are wrong. Emoji can improve digital communications. You could call emoji today's modern hieroglyphics.

Are emoji a language?

English has well over a million words. An adult English speaker will regularly use somewhere between 30,000 and 60,000 words and understand many more. The 800+ emoji available today falls well short of the vocabulary required to express the same number of ideas as a "real" language.

The other feature of a language is its grammar. A language combines words and expressions so that we can express complex ideas ranging from a comment on the weather to a declaration of love.

Sure, emoji can be placed next to one another but they can only communicate a very simple message. For instance, you can't convey international relations using emoji. So emoji can never be a complete language.

Emoji are mainly used to clarify the meaning of a digital message. In spoken language, intonation and gesture provide additional information to the words we speak. For example, we can use intonation to show whether we're asking a question or giving an answer.

In digital communication, emoji fulfil a similar function, enabling the user to add tone and to interpret the meaning of the text.

They also provide a universal language. The three wise monkey emoji means the same in English, Italian or Japanese.

Of course, emoji are also just good fun.

Adapted from "The Conversation"

http://theconversation.com/no-the-rise-of-the-emoji-doesnt-spell-the-end-of-language-42208

Going beyond the chapter

In this chapter you have explored how there are social and formal conventions we should use when we communicate but we can still be creative in our use of language, especially in our use of social media. Now make use of the information you have learned and the communication skills you have developed in this chapter for practical purposes beyond the classroom.

Take action! Some suggestions ...

TED Talks

In this chapter you have learned how to carry out an oral presentation. Why not make your audience bigger and present your ideas on emoji and etiquette to the rest of the school?

Create a TED Talk-style presentation about how social media affect the way that we communicate with each other now or how we will do so in the future. You could work on the presentation you created for either the formative or summative assessments in this chapter.

This presentation could be part of a bigger project and could involve design (IT) and science as well.

Maybe you could put your ideas into a global context. Suggest holding a scientific and technical innovation-themed day/evening where students can discuss issues related to this global context from the perspective of the different subject areas. You could invite the IB Diploma Programme students too as this topic might be relevant for them in their study of theory of knowledge.

Fun reads and creative writing

At the end of this section are suggestions for two books you might be interested in reading: *srsly Hamlet* by William Shakespeare and Courtney Carbone *YOLO Juliet* by William Shakespeare, Courtney Carbone and Brett Wright. These are two famous plays by Shakespeare rewritten in texts, emoji and status updates from characters. After reading these books you might try to write your own version of fairy tales or short stories. Ask your school librarian if they might even keep a copy in the library for other students to read.

Service learning

Speak to your MYP coordinator or action and service coordinator to find out your school's expectations for action and service in your particular grade/year.

The ideas below relate directly to the following service learning outcomes:

- become more aware of your own strengths and areas for growth
- undertake challenges that develop new skills
- discuss, evaluate and plan student-initiated activities
- persevere in action
- work collaboratively with others
- develop international-mindedness through global engagement, multilingualism and intercultural understanding.

Ideas for service

You could write a style guide for new and existing students in the school. A style guide is a set of rules and conventions for writing. An organization, a college or a school uses it to help clarify and set standards for communications.

You might wish to write a guide that can be used by younger students in the school. You could do this together with students who study English Language and Literature and who might also be interested in this topic.

Your guide could cover the following topics:
- how to write formally to teachers

- how to write formally to outside organizations (such as NGOs, charities, local government, etc.)

- the etiquette of blog and comment writing

- how to write polite emails to other students

- a guide to teachers and parents about teenage slang

- the acceptable and unacceptable uses of emoji.

You may wish to include other topics of your own choice.

If your school does not have a style guide already, create a list of useful topics such as:
- guidelines on essay writing

- writing reflections

- writing lab reports, etc.

Then you could approach your school's administration and suggest that such a document would be useful.

If you enjoyed this chapter here are some texts for further reading

- Debra Fine, *Beyond Texting, The Fine Art of Face-to-Face Communication for Teenagers*
- Denise Schipani, *Why Txtng Is OK for Kids* ☺ **http://www.readbrightly.com/why-txtng-is-ok-for-kids/**
- Lauren Myracle, *Internet Girls series: ttyl; ttfn; l8r, g8r; yolo*
- Michelle Skeen, *Communication Skills for Teens: How to Listen, Express, and Connect for Success*
- William Shakespeare and Courtney Carbone, *srsly Hamlet*
- William Shakespeare and Brett Wright, *YOLO Juliet*

ATL **Research and thinking skills**

At the end of any learning experience always ask yourself these questions:

- What lessons have I learned from this chapter?
- What concepts don't I yet understand about this topic?
- What questions do I still have about this topic?

Where can I find answers to these questions?

In context

Global context: Orientation in time and space

What is the meaning of "where" and "when"?

In this chapter we will explore stories that involve personal histories, journeys and turning points. These stories examine discoveries, explorations and migrations. Through the stories we will look at the relationships between individuals and the societies in which they live from personal, local and global perspectives.

The key themes of the chapter are exchanges and interactions between people and how these relationships can evolve and adapt because of new circumstances.

Key concept: Communication

Communication is the exchange or transfer of signals, facts, ideas and symbols. It requires a sender, a message and an intended receiver. Communication involves the activity of conveying information or meaning.

In this chapter we will take the theme of "The Quest" which is one of the most common and important forms of story. By examining "The Quest" as a way of telling a story, we can see how ideas are communicated both in speech and in writing.

Related concept: Function

In this chapter we will look at communicative **function** – the different purposes for which we can use language in the art of storytelling. By examining "The Quest" we can see how writers use different functions such as description and narrative to create stories in both speech and writing.

Statement of inquiry

Stories about quests involve journeys, turning points and realizations. Through these stories we can examine the relationships between individuals and the societies in which they live from personal, local and global perspectives.

Inquiry questions

➔ What is a quest?

➔ Can a story have more than one meaning?

➔ What are the important elements of a quest story?

➔ What and how does audio-visual Text D communicate about the theme of the quest?

➔ Can we use spoken dialogue to improve a quest story?

➔ What elements should a good quest story contain?

What is a quest?

Before you read Text A

Criteria 3Bi, 3Biii

What do you know about quests? Before you begin this chapter, conduct a class brainstorming session on the subject. How many examples of quests can you think of?

What is the difference between a journey and a quest?

Study the picture and the short text and give your opinions. Describe what you can see and what you imagine, using the questions below as prompts. There are no "right" answers, but you should back up your opinions with reasons or evidence.

- Who is the seeker?
- What do you imagine is the character's quest?
- Where has the character come from?
- How long has he/she been traveling?
- Where is the character going?
- Why?
- Is anyone traveling with the character?
- What problems lie ahead?

In a quest story, a powerful character usually asks a younger person to find something valuable. This quest can involve a long journey. Frequently the seeker must then perform a task with the object before he, or she, can return home. Can you think of any stories that follow this pattern?

While you read Text A

Criterion 3Bi

In the exercise below you must fit the correct word into the correct sentence. Before you begin, categorize the words according to their grammatical form: adjective, noun, verb, article, and so on. As you read the text, think about what type of word would fit into the space provided.

Which words go in the gaps (-x-) in the text? Choose the words from the list below. The first one has been done for you.

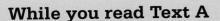

travels	someone	never
lover	the	power
monster	journey	stop
on	magical	wrong
some	hero	between

Text A

The quest is therefore usually about a central figure, or (Ex. hero), trying to achieve an important goal. The object of the quest is often a person or an object that has the (-1-) to change a bad situation. The goal frequently requires a long (-2-).

For example, in a love story a (-3-) seeks the love of a beloved. In fantasy literature the object frequently has (-4-) powers: a ring, a crown, a book, or a stone. The detective story can also be a kind of quest in which (-5-) seeks to uncover the truth.

There are often other characters (-6-) the quest. A teacher or mentor figure often guides (-7-) seeker. A good friend, or a band of travellers, often (-8-) with the seeker. Along this journey the hero will meet a trickster who sends him in the (-9-) direction. The travellers also find other enemies on the way to (-10-) them from reaching their goal.

ATL Research and thinking skills

There are many characters in modern books, films and games that can be seen as going on quests. For example:

- Dorothy in *The Wizard of Oz*
- Frodo in *The Lord of the Rings*
- Sherlock Holmes in the Sherlock Holmes stories and novels
- Bilbo in *The Hobbit*.

The quest is also featured in many popular films. *Star Wars* is a good example.

What other quest stories do you know? Copy and complete the table below.

Hint: cartoon and fairy tale characters often go on quests.

Quest	Seeker	Object of the quest	Journey from/ to	Friend/ companion	Trickster/ enemy

Formative oral and interactive skills: Basic skills for drama

Look at the picture below. Imagine you are the seeker and we are looking at the photograph from your point of view. Work in groups of five or six. First answer these questions and then plan a short dramatic role-play based on the picture and the questions.

- What is the big story here?
- Where are you coming from?
- What are you looking for and why?
- Where is the object or the person you are looking for at the moment?
- How long have you been looking?
- What problems do you face?
- How will you solve your problem?
- What problems have you already overcome?
- How will you get what you are looking for?

Planning and scaffolding

Each participant in the role-play should play a character. In order to be clear, you should work out the roles and personalities for the characters first. If it helps, you can add an additional character to the role-play. First fill in this chart and then make cue cards for each member of your role-play.

	Name and background	Personality	Role in the quest
The seeker			
Celebrity A			
Celebrity B			
The bodyguard			
Journalists and photographers			
Other character:			

Act out your role-play.

Formative writing activity: Basic skills for narrative

Criteria 3Di, 3Dii

Once you have completed the drama and you know how the story ends, use the ideas your group has generated to write up your own short quest story in 200–250 words.

Make sure you:

- give your quest story a title.

- give your story a beginning, middle and ending

- use past tenses

- decide whether to write a first person, "I- focused", story, or a third person, "he/she focused " story.

Planning and scaffolding

Criterion 3Civ

Communicating with a sense of audience

Now think about the language you will use. Think about your audience. Choose one of these registers:

- very formal, as if talking politely to a very important stranger

- formal, as if talking very politely to people you don't know well

- informal, as if talking to a friend.

Planning and scaffolding

Who was the seeker?	Where was the seeker coming from and going to?	What were they looking for and why?	How long was the quest?	Did the seeker have a friend or companions?	What problems did the seeker face?

ATL Thinking skills

Use your creative thinking skills to create an original story.

- Use brainstorming to generate new ideas.

- Consider multiple alternatives.

- Create a novel ending.

- Make unexpected or unusual connections.

- Make guesses, ask "what if" questions and generate testable hypotheses.

Conclusion to factual question

What is a quest?

Having examined this section, what is your answer to the question?

Can a story have more than one meaning?

Before you read Text B

The title of the next quest story is "The Moth and The Star" by James Thurber. It is a modern fairy tale.

The story is a **fable**. In other words, it is a story that is symbolic. One the one hand it has a **surface meaning**; it is a simple story of a moth and a star. However, fables are used to prove a point about a real-life situation. There is usually a moral, or point, at the end of the story. Therefore, the story is also symbolic. In a fable, the writer uses animals to suggest human characters or character types. All the elements, such as the various characters and star, represent a different idea. Make a list of fables you know. List both the name of the fable and the moral of the story.

This story is a quest.

Can you predict what the storyline could be? Use these prompts to guide you.

- Quest?
- Seeker?
- Object of the quest?

- Journey from/to?
- Friend/companion?
- Trickster/enemy?

ATL Research and thinking skills

Use your intercultural understanding to interpret stories

Frequently, variations on same stories exist in different cultures. Sometimes the setting is different; sometimes the characters have different names. However, the underlying story and the moral is often the same. Why is this? What does this tell you about fables, folk stories and fairy stories? Do you think that the existence of these stories points towards a shared set of human values?

ATL Research and social skills

The story is a fable. In other words, it is a story that is symbolic.

1 Make a list of fables you know. List both the name of the fable and the moral of the story.

2 What are the common characteristics of the fables you have listed?

3 Make a list of the shared features of these fables. You may want to think about these elements of the stories.

    A The type of narrator

    B The characters in the fable

    C The setting of the story

    D The beginning

    E The structure of the story

    F The ending

After reading Text B

How accurate were your predictions?

See if your predictions were correct. What did you get right and what did you get wrong? Now that you have read the story, answer the questions again.

- What was the quest?
- Who was the seeker?
- What was the object of the quest?
- Where did the seeker journey from/to?
- Who was the friend/companion?
- Who was the trickster/enemy?

Text B

The Moth and the Star

A young and impressionable moth once 1
set his heart on a certain star. He told his
mother about this and she counselled him to
set his heart on a bridge lamp instead. "Stars
aren't the thing to hang around," she said; 5
"lamps are the thing to hang around." "You
get somewhere that way," said the moth's
father. "You don't get anywhere chasing
stars."

But the moth would not heed the words of 10
either parent. Every evening at dusk when
the star came out he would start flying
toward it and every morning at dawn he
would crawl back home worn out with his
vain endeavour. One day his father said to 15
him, "You haven't burned a wing in months,
boy, and it looks to me as if you were never
going to. All your brothers have been badly
burned flying around street lamps and all
your sisters have been terribly singed flying 20
around house lamps. Come on, now, get
yourself scorched! A big strapping moth like
you without a mark on him!"

The moth left his father's house, but he
would not fly around street lamps and he 25
would not fly around house lamps. He went
right on trying to reach the star, which was
four and one-third light years, or twenty-
five trillion miles, away. The moth thought
it was just caught in the top branches of an 30
elm. He never did reach the star, but he went
right on trying, night after night, and when

he was a very, very old moth he began to think that he really had reached the star and he went around saying so. This gave him a deep and lasting pleasure, and he lived to a great old age. His parents and his brothers and his sisters had all been burned to death when they were quite young.

Moral: Who flies afar from the sphere of our sorrow is here today, and here tomorrow.   40

James Thurber, *Fables for our Time*

Text handling: Factual assessment of Text B

Criteria 3Bi, 3Bii

1 **True/false**

Read the text carefully and identify which of the statements below are true and which are false. Justify each answer with a relevant brief quotation from Text B. Both a correct identification and a quotation are required for one mark.

		True	False
Example:	The moth's quest was to reach the star.	✔	
Justification	"set his heart on a certain star"		
1	His mother did not support his quest.		
Justification:			
2	She told the young moth to fly to a candle.		
Justification:			
3	The father thought the star was impossible to reach.		
Justification:			
4	The moth didn't listen to his parents' advice.		
Justification:			
5	Once a week the moth tried to fly to the star.		
Justification:			
6	Eventually, his brothers and sisters tried to fly to the star too.		
Justification:			
7	The moth finally reached the star.		
Justification:			
8	The moth has a much longer life than his brothers and sisters.		
Justification:			

Referencing: grammar in context

In this exercise you have to identify precise references of key words or phrases in the text.

Complete the following table by indicating to whom or to what the word(s) underlined refer(s). Write your answers on a separate sheet of paper.

In the phrase ...	the word(s)	refer(s) to ...
Example: He told his mother about <u>this</u> (*line* 7)	"this"	his quest to fly to the star
9. You get somewhere <u>that way</u> (line 9)	"that way"	
10. he would start flying toward <u>it</u> (line 13)	"it"	

② **Multiple-choice questions**

Choose the correct answer from A, B, C, or D.

11. The father did not agree with the moth's ambitions because he thought:
  A. the moth was not working hard enough
  B. the moth wanted to get burned
  C. the moth should be doing the same as everyone else
  D. he disliked his brothers and sisters. ☐

12. As an adult the moth thought the star was:
  A. four and one-third light years away
  B. next to the street lamps
  C. in the top of a tree
  D. twenty-five trillion miles away. ☐

13. When the moth was very old he:
  A. said he had wasted his life
  B. believed he had achieved his ambition
  C. missed his brothers and sisters
  D. told everyone about the star. ☐

14. In the fable the moth's siblings died young because:
  A. they wanted to be like everyone else in society
  B. they followed their parents' advice
  C. they lacked the imagination to try something different
  D. only people who are strong individuals can be successful.
  E. All of the above. ☐

Thinking and social skills   Criterion 3Bii

In groups discuss the answers to the questions below. When you have finished, brainstorm the lessons that can be learned from this fable and present your answers to the class.

1   The quest story *The Moth and The Star* has a **literal** meaning but under the surface it also has a much more important **symbolic** meaning. As the writer says, "Who flies afar from the sphere of our sorrow is here today, and here tomorrow."

The moral of this story suggests:

A.   we should always run away from unhappiness
B.   we should not follow our parents' advice
C.   always try, even if the dream is impossible
D.   not tell the truth about our achievements.

2   The story is a **symbolic quest**. Each character and object represents an idea.
Find the possible meanings of these symbolic elements of the story:

A.   the moth
B.   the moth's brothers and sisters
C.   the street and house lamps
D.   the moth's parents
E.   the star
F.   the quest for the star

Discussion and debate

Do you agree with the moral of the story, The Moth and the Star: "Who flies afar from the sphere of our sorrow is here today, and here tomorrow"?.

Do your ambitions take you further than your friends and family, your hometown, your home country?

Or do you think it best to stay close to home, friends and family, and try to be like everyone else?

Discuss the question and see what conclusions you come to. Share your ideas with the rest of your class.

Oral and interactive skills: Drama   Criterion 3Ci

Study the picture opposite.

Describe the photograph in detail.

Be prepared to make some guesses.

Who are these three people?

Give the three peoples names and identities.

What is their relationship?

Where are they?

What is happening?

What has happened before this scene?

What are they saying to each other?

What do you think will happen next?

Imagine the girl in the picture above on page 203 has just won a scholarship to spend a year in an international school in another country. This is her quest. However, her father is strongly against the idea. Her mother is trying to see both points of view.

In groups, create a mini-drama with the following characters:

Father – against the idea

Student – in favour of a year abroad

Mother – neither for nor against the idea

- What will be the moral of your drama?

- What lessons will it teach the audience?

- How many meanings will your story have?

- What will be the the literal meaning?

- What will be the deeper, symbolic meaning?

You may use very informal or emotional language as you are speaking in a family context.

Planning and scaffolding

Discuss in [Criteria 3Cii, 3Ciii] your groups whether it is good idea for the girl to go abroad for a year. Agree on five or more reasons to go, and five or more reasons why it may not be such a good idea.

ATL Self-management and social skills

Here is an opportunity to prepare for summative assessments.

You have been given a learning goal that is challenging but realistic: to create a mini-drama

Plan your play script. Decide what each character would say. Write it up, adding stage directions as necessary.

Provide a script for each character so that each person knows what to say.

Present the information as a drama script that is easily understandable.

Here is also an opportunity to show that you can manage your time and a task effectively.

Give yourself a deadline for completion of the task.

Here are some useful social skills you can develop during this exercise.

As you plan the role-play and rehearse it work together by:
- listening actively to other perspectives and ideas

- encouraging everyone to contribute

- helping all members of the group to succeed

- giving and receiving meaningful feedback.

Formative writing activity response to Text B: Writing a narrative from different perspectives

Criteria 3Di, 3Dii

Once you have completed your discussions, use the ideas you have discussed in this section to write one or two versions of the quest story.

- You could retell "The Moth and the Star" first from the moth's point of view (first-person narrative), and then from the point of view one of the people the old moth tells his story to.

- Alternatively, write up the story of the girl who wanted to study abroad. You could first write from the girl's point of view (first-person narrative) and then from the father's or mother's point of view, (third person).

Write about 200 to 250 words for each version and give each of your stories a title. The narrative will contain a protagonist, a quest and at least two other characters. The storyline should contain a conflict with a clear beginning, middle and end. Will you write in the first person or the third person?

Planning and scaffolding

Criteria 3Dii, 3Civ, 3Diii

- Give your story a beginning, middle and ending.
- Use past tenses.
- Give your story a title.
- Like James Thurber, the author of The Moth and The Star, create a moral to show the underlying meaning of your story. Write the moral at the end of the story.

Planning and scaffolding

Criterion 3Diii

Communicating with a sense of audience

Now think about the language you will use in the story. Will you write using:

A. formal language
B. informal language
C. technical language
D. poetic language
E. a combination of any of these? If so, explain.

Conclusion to the conceptual question

Can a story have more than one meaning?

Having examined this section, what is your answer to the question? Do all stories have both literal and symbolic meaning? Give examples from the stories you have read and created in this section.

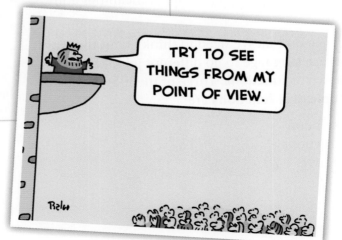

205

Key and related concepts: Communication and function

Communication is the basis of what makes us human and it creates bridges between communities across the globe; it is the essence of Language Acquisition. Effective communication requires a common language (which may be written, spoken or non-verbal). In the case of this course the common language is English.

Communication involves the exchange or transfer of signals, facts, ideas and symbols. It requires a sender, a message and an intended receiver. As you read this, we, the authors, are sending a message to you. As you receive the message, you will interpret it and make sense of it!

All the texts you read and write for this course also need a sender, a message and an intended receiver. An email is a great example of this process.

Communication also involves the act of conveying and receiving information and meanings. In this book you are learning to understand, process and transform information, facts, ideas, meanings and opinions.

In order to do that we need to think about the ways we can use language to do different jobs. These jobs are known as **functions**. Three of the most basic **communicative functions** are:

- description
- instructions
- narrative.

ATL Social and communication skills

In small groups study this diagram, which has come from a computer manual. What does it seem to say about:

A. the way ideas are communicated

B. how computers translate information from one language to another?

- Discuss and come to some conclusion about the meaning of the diagram.

- Think about what you have learned about how information is communicated.

- Discuss what each symbol and colour could mean.

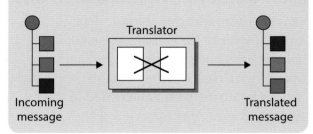

Thinking about communication and function in stories

The function of narrative is to communicate things that have happened. We structure narratives by putting these events into a time sequence, or chronological order. Therefore, narrative is the basis for storytelling.

The narrative makes sense of past events by dividing them into specific events. When we give our narratives a beginning, middle and end, our stories have greater meaning. There is a big difference between:

> She grew up. She married. She had children.

and

> She had children. She married. She grew up.

From the story "The Moth and the Star" write down five or more narrative sentences. You may find it helpful to complete the chart below.

	Character A	did	what/who/where/why
Ex:	The young moth	saw	a star.
1.			
2.			
3.			
4.			
5.			

Description

When we communicate we can also use description. We describe when we want to give details about people, places, things and events. Sometimes we describe through our five senses: sight, sound, smell, taste and touch. We can also describe our emotions when we experience people and things.

Description can be communicated **directly** through the choice of vocabulary such as adjectives and adverbs. Nouns and verbs too can have descriptive qualities.

Descriptive detail can help to create the tone and atmosphere in a text.

Unlike narrative, description is not dependent on a specific order of the sentences.

Copy and fill in the table below, then write short descriptions of the three characters.

	Appearance	Personality	Behaviour towards others
Character A			
Character B			
Character C			

Instructions

Instructions tell, or suggest, what to do or how to act. In a story a character can suggest a series of actions to another. For example, in "The Moth and the Star", the father says, "Come on, now, get yourself scorched." This means the moth should try something dangerous or adventurous.

The relationships between reader and writer can be seen in the way the speaker or writer modifies instructions. What is the relationship between the speaker and the listener in each of the examples below?

Instructions, suggestions or commands?

1. Command   Do it!
2. Instruction   Do it this way.
3. Advice   It would be good to do it like this.
4. Suggestion   I suggest you do it.
5. Hint   You might wish to do it.

Copy and complete the table below with instructions that characters from the story "The Moth and the Star" might have given.

	Character A		Character B	Instruction
1.	The father	said to	the moth	"Go out and have fun."
2.	The mother	said to	the moth	
3.	His brothers and sisters	said to	the moth	
4.	The star	seemed to say to	the moth	
5.	The moth	learned the lesson that it is better to		

Formative oral and interactive skills: Drama

A drama is an imaginary situation in which students play either themselves or imaginary characters. In a Language Acquisition class we can learn how to understand a set of characters, and understand their point of view. We can also use drama to better understand certain ideas, such as a quest or a search.

The conventions of a drama script

The introduction to a play script consists of:

- **Title:** The name of the drama
- **Scene:** Where and when the scene is set
- **Characters:** A list of characters in the scene at the start. You could give some information that we need to know about them, such as age, occupation or relationship with another character.

> *Example*
> Mary, aged 15
> Liz, aged 45, Mary's mother
> Richard, aged 30, a salesman

The actual play script consists of two basic elements:

- **Dialogue** is what the characters say. The name of the character who is speaking should be written on the left-hand side of the page (in the margin). It is a good idea to print it in capitals. Then write a colon.

- **Stage directions** are instructions for the actors. They should be written in brackets (…).

  Example:

The Quest for the Missing Book of Charms

Scene: A forest

Characters:

SUZANNE, a girl, about 13

MARLA, an old woman

(MARLA *is looking for something and talking to herself quietly.* SUZANNE *enters and watches for a while*.)

SUZANNE: What are you doing?

MARLA (surprised): I was looking for my bag. (*Angrily*) Why do want to know?

SUZANNE: I'm sorry. I didn't mean to be nosy.

(SUZANNE *sees MARLA's bag on the ground and picks it up*.)

SUZANNE: Here it is!

MARLA (Sharply): Give it to me now!

SUZANNE: There is no need to be rude. You would think there was something really valuable inside.

MARLA: There is!

Etc.

Discussion and debate

Prose is the ordinary form of language we use for everyday language. We use prose for writing stories.

In groups sketch out the scene opposite as a story written in prose.

Think about the conventions of a drama script. How is your text, written in prose, different to a drama script?

Make a list of differences.

Think about the functions of the two text types. Why is a drama script different to prose?

ATL Social and communication skills   Criteria 3Cii, 3Ciii, 3Civ

Earlier in the chapter, you made up a quest story. Now, in groups, create a drama script from the same material. Write one or two scenes. Use the conventions from the example above. Alternatively:

- Retell your own version of "The Moth and the Star".

- Retell the story of the girl who wants to study abroad.

- Create a quest story of your own. Choose a scene or a couple of scenes to dramatize. They could be moments of success, failure, disappointment, loss and loneliness; your drama could present an argument or a fight.

- Decide which characters will take part in the scene and what will happen.

  o Who is the seeker?

  o Where is the seeker coming from and going to?

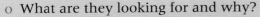

o What are they looking for and why?

o How long will the quest take?

o Does the seeker have a friend or companions?

o What problems does the seeker face?

- Now work out what the characters will say to each other.

- After having listened to each other's ideas, work out a final version that you will present in front of the class.

- Think about how the characters will talk to each other.

- You may use very informal language as you are speaking in a family context. However, make sure that the language is appropriate for the classroom.

- Make a set of notes on cue cards that you can use to act out the scene.

When you are ready, you can act out your script in front of your class. Alternatively, video yourselves.

Formative writing skills: Narrative quest story   Criteria 3Di, 3Dii, 3Diii

A narrative story amuses or entertains its readers with actual or imaginary events. It is usually written in prose.

The **storyteller** is usually either an outsider telling the story (a third-person narrator) or a character who takes part in the action (a first-person narrator).

A quest story has a clear plot structure:

1. The reason to search for the important object

2. Setting off

3. The journey

4. Problems along the way

5. The finding of the object

6. A fight

7. An ending with a moral

Now look at the pictures on the next page. Use your imagination and your creativity to invent your own quest narrative.

Creating a quest narrative from a picture stimulus

Criteria 3Di 3Dii

A

B

C

Look at the three pictures A, B and C on page 212 and use one or more of them as the basis for a story about a quest. The narrative will contain a protagonist, a quest and at least two other characters. The storyline should contain a conflict with a clear beginning, middle and end.

Plot

You may find it helpful to copy and complete the chart below.

What will be the **object** of the quest?	
Who will be the **seeker(s)**?	
What **instructions** does the seeker receive?	
What is the **conflict**?	
What will be the **climax** to the narrative?	
What is the **resolution** of the conflict?	
What will be the **message** of the story?	

Will you write from:

A. a first-person point of view

B. a third-person point of view?

Will you write using:

A. formal language

B. informal language

C. technical language

D. poetic language

E. a combination of any of these? If so, explain.

ATL Thinking and self-management skills

By creating your own story you have an opportunity to use your creative thinking skills. You will be able to generate new ideas and consider them from new perspectives.

Create a plan of action to complete the task on time.

- Plan the assignment; meet your deadlines.
- Use a planner to timetable the assignment.
- Set realistic goals and timescales.
- Plan strategies and take action to achieve your goals.
- Use appropriate strategies for organizing information.

ATL Thinking skills

Use your creativity to develop ideas for your story.

- Create novel solutions to authentic problems. What quest do the photos suggest?

- Make guesses, ask "what if" questions and generate testable hypotheses

- Use brainstorming and visual diagrams to generate new ideas

- Make unexpected or unusual connections between the three photos.

- Consider new perspectives. Which of the characters in the picture do you identify with?

  Who are the other characters in the photos?

- Consider multiple alternatives. Will you write in the first person or third person?

What are the important elements of a quest story?

Before reading Text C

Criterion 3Bii

Elements of a story

It would seem that many stories, such as quests, are common to all cultures and all times in our history. All stories have two important elements: the **storyteller** and the **plot**.

A storyteller who is inside the story can tell a narrative. This is **the first-person point of view**: "I came. I saw. I conquered" (Julius Caesar). Alternatively, narrative can be told from a person outside the story. The storyteller explains what happened to other people. This is **the third-person point of view**: "He never did reach the star, but he went right on trying" (James Thurber, "The Moth and the Star"). The **second-person point of view** involves talking directly to the reader, "You walk into the room with a pencil in your hand" (Bob Dylan, "Ballad of a Thin Man").

See the chart below for details.

Point of View	Pronouns	Description
First person	I, me, my, mine, we, us, our, ours	It's all about me.
Second person	You, your, yours	You're talking directly to the reader.
Third person	He, she, it, they, them, their, etc.	Outside point of view.

Make a list of the books you have read recently. Categorize them according to the point of view from which they are written. Which style, if any, do you prefer? Why?

The plot is the storyline. In order for the story to work there has to be some **conflict**. The conflict is usually caused by an argument or contest. This moment is called the **inciting incident**. The conflict makes the story go forward until there is a **climax**. The conflict is solved at the end of the story – **a resolution**.

Pick one famous story.

Identify:

A. the conflict

B. the inciting incident

C. the climax

D. the resolution.

Does this plot line work for all the stories you know?

Discussion and debate

Themes

Criteria 3Dii, 3Diii

Here are five themes found in fairy stories. Now brainstorm a list of fairy stories. Match the fairy stories to these five themes.

1. Quests

Many fairy tales are about growing up and overcoming difficulties. The characters are sent on a journey and they must successfully complete their quest in order to come home.

2. Transformation

Frogs can become princes, princes become beasts, serving girls become princesses, and puppets become real boys.

3. Justice

Most fairy tales have a strong sense of justice. They tell of the fight between good and evil. At the end the wicked are punished and the good are rewarded.

4. Rags to riches

Some fairy tales are stories about very poor children who become rich. Such children often have a magical helper or a mentor.

5. Intelligence

Fairy tale characters often need to outsmart their older or more powerful antagonists, rivals or enemies.

The hero or heroine

All quest stories have a central hero or heroine who goes on a search. They frequently share similar characteristics. For instance, they are often loners or outsiders. Sometimes they are orphans. At the beginning of the story they are often powerless or lack knowledge.

Look at this visual of four young heroes and discuss the similarities in situation and character between these popular heroes from modern-day quests. Alternatively, you may wish to use other heroes or heroines as examples. Study the chart below and then fill in your answers.

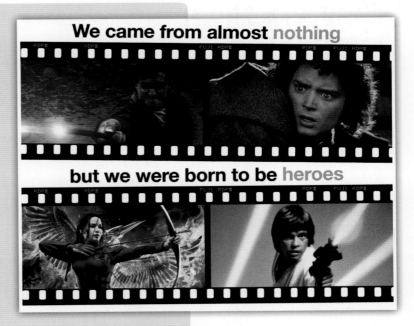

We came from almost nothing
but we were born to be heroes

	Personal situation	Character and characteristics	Background to the story	Their quest
Harry Potter				
Bilbo Baggins				
Katniss Everdeen				
Luke Skywalker				
Other (Name)				

What other similarities can you find?

Another very common element of the story is the **list of supporting characters**. We can often find the same character types, (villain, rival friend, mentor/teacher, beloved, companions) in many stories.

Think of two well-known stories and identify the different elements of the story. Study and complete the chart below.

	Story A	Story B
Storyteller		
Plot		
Characters		
Conflict		
Climax		
Resolution		
Theme/message		

Before you read Text C
Prediction

"The guitar player" is a modern variation on the quest story. Two rivals are in love with the same girl. Therefore, the story is a quest for love. The girl, who is the guitar player in the title, is the object of the quest. However, the story has a twist – a surprise ending. What do you think might happen? Use your imagination to brainstorm possible endings. Share your ideas in class.

Now read the story and find out which idea is closest to. the actual ending of the story.

Text C

The guitar player

A girl played on her guitar and it so happened that someone passing by listened and fell in love with her. "Is it my music you love," inquired the girl, "or me?" The music continued, water from a fountain rose into the air and fell away. The listener thought hard and finally said, "I don't know. What is the right answer?"

"Shan't tell you," replied the girl, "but that's not it," and she went on playing.

Soon another passer-by happened to see her and also fell in love. "Is it me you love," inquired the girl, "or my guitar?" The second passer-by stared at the guitar, smiled at the girl and at last ventured to say, "Well, I don't know. It's a beautiful instrument. What is the right answer?" But she just said that that wasn't it, and went on playing.

The two passers-by were greatly perplexed. All night long the guitar music ran through their heads, and when they returned the next day it was perfectly obvious that they had prepared their speeches.

"I would love you," declared the first, "even if you could not play a note of the music."

"And I would love you," swore the second, "even if you did not own a guitar."

"You don't understand," replied the girl. "I am a musician. Which me do you love, if you do not care about my music at all?"

"Oh," they said. "Did we give you the wrong answer?"

"Yes," replied the girl.

"Well, what is the right answer?"

"You must love me altogether; just as I am, all my gifts, all my possessions, everything I've been and ever shall be from now on."

"But that's impossible!" they cried out together.

"Yes," agreed the girl and chose a sad little tune to suit the occasion.

Sunjita Namjoshi

After reading Text C

Short-answer questions

Answer the following questions. Write your answers on a separate sheet of paper.

1. What attracted the first passer-by to the guitar player?

2. What question did the girl ask the first passer-by?

3. What attracted the second passer-by to the guitar player?

4. What question did the girl ask to the second passer-by?

5. What answer did both passers-by give?

6. Why did the girl say she was rejecting both lovers on the second day?

7. What is the girl looking for in a lover?

8. Suggest a possible meaning for the phrase, "(she) chose a sad little tune to suit the occasion"?

2 **Multiple-choice questions**

Choose the correct answer from A, B, C, or D.

9. The **plot** is a quest for:
    A. beauty
    B. love
    C. music
    D. money. ☐

10. Stories often deal with some **conflict**. The conflict in "The guitar player" is the conflict between:
    A. the two lovers
    B. the lovers and the guitar player
    C. the lovers and society in which they live
    D. the lovers and nature. ☐

11. What is the main **theme** of the story?
    A. Music is more important than love.
    B. Love is more important than music.
    C. Love means knowing what a person likes.
    D. Love means accepting a person for what she is. ☐

12. The **storyteller** writes from:
    A. a first-person point of view
    B. a second-person point of view
    C. a third-person point of view
    D. a fourth-person point of view. ☐

13. The conflict is **resolved** when:
    A. the girl keeps her independence
    B. the girl chooses one of the lovers
    C. the lovers resolve their conflict
    D. one of the lovers wins. ☐

Thinking and communication skills

Working in pairs answer these question.

1   In what ways is "The guitar player" a typical quest story?

2   In what ways is it different to a typical quest?

Once you have agreed on your ideas, complete the table below. Present your conclusions to class.

	Similarities	Differences
The object of the quest		
The "heroes"		
The plot/storyline		
The outcome of the quest		
The message		
Other elements of the quest		

Formative oral and interactive skills: Drama

Criteria 3Cii, 3Ciii, 3Civ

Planning and scaffolding

Use the ideas on drama earlier in the chapter to help you plan your work.

Create your own version of "The guitar player"

Choose one scene from the story "The guitar player" and create a drama script for it.

- Make a set of notes on cue cards that you can use to act out the scene.

- Decide which characters will take part in the scene and what will happen. Now work out what the characters will say to each other.

- After having listened to each other's ideas, work out a final version that you will present in front of the class.

- Think about how the characters will talk to each other.

- You may use very informal language as you are speaking in a family context. However, make sure that the language is appropriate for the classroom.

Formative writing activity: Story writing

Now write up your own prose version of "The guitar player". You could tell your story from a different point of view:

A. the girl

B. one of the lovers

C. someone else – an observer.

Write between 200 and 250 words. The narrative should contain a protagonist, a quest and at least two other characters. The storyline should contain a conflict with a clear beginning, middle and end. Decide whether to write in the first person or the third person.

Planning and scaffolding

Copy the table below and use it to help to formulate your ideas.

	Your version of "The guitar player"
Who will be the storyteller?	
Will it be a first-person or third-person narrative?	
Will your story be a quest or some other kind of plot?	
Which characters will be in the story?	
What is the conflict?	
What will be the climax to the narrative?	
What is the resolution of the conflict?	
Where will the narrative begin?	
How will the narrative end?	
What will be the moral of the story?	

Planning and scaffolding   Criterion 3Diii

Communicating with a sense of audience

Now think about the language you will use in the story. Choose one of these registers:

- very formal, as if talking politely to a very important stranger.
- formal, as if talking very politely to people you don't know well
- informal, as if talking to a friend.

Conclusion to the conceptual question

What are the important elements of a quest story?

Having examined this section, what is your answer to the question?

What and how does audio-visual Text D communicate about the theme of the quest?

Conceptual question

Before you watch Text D

What do we know so far?

In this chapter you have looked into the topic of the quest. As a class, make a list of the most important ideas you have learned so far in your investigations.

At this stage, are there any points you don't understand?

Make a list of your questions.

How many answers can you find in this audio-visual section?

Suggested texts for this section

Here are some videos of fictional and real-life quests. Choose one and then answer the questions below.

A. **https://www.youtube.com/watch?v=mx1XZoPgNlU**

An Afghan boy looks for a new life in the UK

B. **https://www.youtube.com/watch?v=yJzcQ607sFQ**

Leonard Nimoy's documentary: *In Search of the Loch Ness Monster*

C. **https://www.youtube.com/watch?v=wZdpNglLbt8**

The trailer to *Finding Nemo*

Alternatively, watch a video of a narrative quest of your choosing. Respond to the tasks and answer the questions in the appropriate manner. Write your answers on a separate sheet of paper.

Before you watch Text D

Focusing activity

Read through the exercises below to make sure you know what to look and listen for. You may need to watch the material several times and discuss possible answers in class after each viewing and listening.

While you watch Text D

Choose one of the short narrative videos listed above. Respond to the tasks and answer the questions in the appropriate manner.

1. This audio-visual stimulus seems to be related to which of these MYP global contexts?

    A. Identities and relationships

    B. Orientation in space and time

    C. Personal and cultural expression

    D. Scientific and technical innovation

    E. Globalization and sustainability

    F. Fairness and development

2. Summarize the main points of the stimulus. You may find it useful to copy and complete the table below, adding extra supporting points if necessary. You will need the answers to these questions to help you complete the planning and scaffolding of the oral and interactive skills exercise below.

ATL Research skills

Media Literacy

In this section you can develop these valuable 21st century learning skills.

* Interacting with media to use and create ideas and information.

* Making informed choices about personal viewing experiences.

* Understanding the impact of media representations.

* Seeking a range of perspectives from varied sources.

* Communicating information and ideas effectively.

	The story you watched
What is the title?	
Who is the storyteller?	
Is it a first-person or third-person narrative?	
Where does the narrative begin?	
What kind of quest does the video narrate?	
What characters are featured in the story?	
What is the conflict?	
What is the climax to the narrative?	
What, if any, is the resolution of the conflict?	
How does the video end?	
What is the message of the story?	

1 Multiple-choice questions with justifications

3. The approach to the subject matter of the audio-visual stimulus is mainly:

    A. entertaining   **C.** persuasive

    B. factual   **D.** other. ☐

    Justification/reason:

4. How would you describe the content of the stimulus?

    A. Really interesting   **C.** Fairly interesting

    B. Interesting   **D.** Uninteresting ☐

    Justification/reason:

2 **Multiple-choice questions**

Answer questions 5–10.

5. What was the format of the audio-visual stimulus?
   A. Speech
   B. Conversation/discussion
   C. Debate
   D. Documentary
   E. Other:

6. The purpose of the audio-visual stimulus was to:
   A. narrate a story
   B. describe a situation
   C. explain a problem
   D. argue a point of view
   E. give instructions/guidelines
   F. other:

7. How many points of view did the audio-visual stimulus show?
   A. One
   B. Two
   C. Three
   D. More than three

8. The opinions in the audio-visual stimulus are:
   A. very balanced
   B. quite balanced
   C. biased
   D. very one-sided

9. How much did the audio-visual stimulus use graphics?
   A. A lot
   B. More than twice
   C. Once or twice
   D. Never

10. Which of these techniques are used in the audio-visual stimulus?
    A. Voiceover
    B. Special lighting techniques
    C. Music and sound effects
    D. Other special effects
    E. None of the above
    F. All of the above
    G. Some of the above

Formative interactive oral: Retell the story as a drama

Criterion 3Aiii

The purpose of this drama is to show an understanding of the story and the elements of storytelling shown in the video you have watched.

Planning and scaffolding

As a group, make sure you have an overview of your quest story by completing the following table.

	Your quest
Storyteller	
Plot	
Characters	
Conflict	
Climax	
Resolution	
Theme/message	

ATL Social and self-management skills

This task is a major opportunity to show that you can work cooperatively in a group to collaborate on a complex set of ideas and create and communicate many of the ideas in this chapter. The task will also give you an opportunity to practise the skills you will need for the summative oral and interactive assessment.

Decide which scene(s) to dramatize. Choose from the following list of moments in the plot structure.

- The reason to search for the important object
- Setting off
- The journey
- Problems along the way
- The finding of the object
- A fight
- An ending with a moral

Now make some more decisions.

- Decide which characters will take part in the scene and what will happen. Work out what the characters will say to each other. Note these ideas in a basic script.

- Think about how the characters will talk to each other. You may use very informal language as you are speaking in a family context. However, make sure that the language is appropriate for the classroom.

The quest for love perhaps?

- After having listened to each other's ideas, work on a final version of the script that you will present in front of the class.

- Use the conventions of a drama script (title, setting, characters. dialogue and stage directions) to sketch out your drama script.

- Make sure you have any props (objects used on stage by actors during a performance, for example, fake weapons, books, treasure chest, magic wands) you need before you act out your drama.

> **Planning and scaffolding**
>
> Use your answers from question 2 above to provide information and background for your drama.

Formative writing activity   Criterion 3Aiii

Rewrite the basic plot of the film you have watched.

Use your answers from question 2 above, your scaffolding notes, and the drama you have produced to write a short narrative of 200–250 words. The narrative will contain a protagonist, a quest and at least two other characters. The storyline should contain a conflict with a clear beginning, an inciting incident, middle with a climax and end with a resolution.

The task will also give you an opportunity to practise the skills you will need for the summative written assessment at the end of this section.

> **Planning and scaffolding**   Criterion 3Diii
>
> **Communicating with a sense of audience**
>
> Decide whether you will write your narrative in the first person or the third person.
>
> Also think about the language you will use in the story. Choose one of these registers:
>
> • very formal, as if talking politely to a very important stranger
> • formal, as if talking very politely to people you don't know well
> • informal, as if talking to a friend.

Conclusion to the conceptual question

What and how does audio-visual Text D communicate about the theme of the quest?

Having examined this section, what is your answer to the question?

ATL Research and self-management skills

Have you found answers to all the questions you asked at the beginning of this section? If not, where, and how, do you think you could find the information you are seeking?

Summative activities

In this summative assessment you will have an opportunity to show your understanding of the topic of the quest. You will also be assessed on your use of the communication skills you have developed in this chapter. To complete the assessment you will undertake two tasks related to the statement of inquiry for this chapter. Each assessment task requires you to answer a debatable question.

Statement of inquiry

Stories about quests involve journeys, turning points and realizations. Through these stories we can examine the relationships between individuals and the societies in which they live from personal, local and global perspectives.

Debatable question 1

Can we use spoken dialogue to improve a quest story?

Debatable question 2

What elements should a good quest story contain?

For the first task, you will watch a video and create a drama based on the contents. To answer the second question, you will read a text and produce a narrative based on the contents.

Summative oral task: Presentation

Debatable question 1: Can we use spoken dialogue to improve a quest story?

Watch the following video ("The Quest"). As you watch, decide whether the video is a good example of a quest story, or not. You may wish to add material to improve the quest plotline.

Choose up to three scenes from the video involving one or more elements of the hero's quest. This could be the section of the journey, one or more encounters, or a realization or a turning point in the plot. By adding dialogue and stage directions, you should first create a rough draft of a script to be acted out in class or to be recorded.

The script should help the audience understand the scene's place in the plot and the character of the hero.

The script should take 3 or 4 minutes to act out.

Note: you will be assessed on the spoken performance, not on the script itself.

Text E

The Quest

https://www.youtube.com/watch?v=s6cbhk2Et4I

You have had opportunities to practise producing and presenting drama scripts throughout this unit. In this summative assessment you will have an opportunity to show your understanding of the following learning objectives:

Criterion A: Comprehending spoken and visual text

3Ai   *Show understanding of information, main ideas and supporting details, and draw conclusions*

3Aii *Interpret conventions*

3Aiii *Engage with the spoken and visual text by identifying ideas, opinions and attitudes and by making a response to the text based on personal experiences and opinions*

Criterion C: Communicating in response to spoken and/or written and/or visual text

3Ci   *Respond appropriately to spoken and/or written and/or visual text*

3Cii *Interact in rehearsed and unrehearsed exchanges*

3Ciii *Express ideas and feelings, and communicate information in familiar and some unfamiliar situations*

3Civ *Communicate with a sense of audience and purpose*

Criterion D: Using language in spoken and/or written form

3Di   *Write and/or speak using a range of vocabulary, grammatical structures and conventions; when speaking, use clear pronunciation and intonation*

3Dii *Organize information and ideas and use a range of basic cohesive devices*

3Diii *Use language to suit the context*

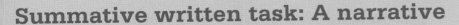

Summative written task: A narrative

In this summative assessment you will have another opportunity to show your understanding of the topic of the quest. You will demonstrate the written communication skills you have developed in this chapter. To complete the assessment you will undertake another task related to the statement of inquiry for this chapter.

Debatable question 2: What elements should a good quest story contain?

The text below outlines different forms of quests used in video gaming. Imagine you are going to write a new storyline for a video games company. Create a narrative based on one of the types of quest described in the text. Make sure you identify clearly which kind of quest you have created. Use language appropriate to the audience. The best answers will contain all the important elements of a quest. Write between 200 and 250 words.

Text F

Video gaming: Quests

A quest in role-playing video games … is a task that a player-controlled character, or group of characters, may complete in order to gain a reward. Rewards may include an increase in the character's experience in order to learn new skills and abilities, treasure such as gold coins, access to new locations or areas, or any combination of the above…

In the most general sense, a quest is a "hunt for a specific outcome", in contrast to simply winning a game. Typical quests involve killing a set number of creatures or collecting a list of specific items. Some quests may take only a few minutes or hours to complete, while others may take several days or weeks. It is common for a quest to require characters to have met a certain set of conditions before they are allowed to begin. Often, the larger the reward, the longer the quest takes to finish…

A *side-quest* is an optional section of a video game, and is commonly found in role-playing video games. It is a smaller mission within a larger storyline, and can be used as a means to provide non-linear structures to an otherwise linear plot. As a general rule, the completion of side-quests is not essential for the game to be finished, but can bring various benefits to the player characters.

Types of quest

Quests are typically grouped into one of four categories: kill quests, gather quests, delivery quests and escort quests.

Kill quests

A *kill quest* sends the character out to kill either a specific number of named creatures, or a specific non-player character or NPC. These types of quests often require the character to bring back proof of their work, such as trophies, or body parts (boar tusks, wolf pelts, etc.).

Combo quests

The *combo quest* requires a player to attack certain enemies or structures with a combination of attacks until the required number of combos has been reached. Enemies in these quests are usually either immortal or infinite in number till the player is successful in which case the enemies would be killed or stop appearing.

Delivery quests

Another type of quest is the *delivery quest* … or fetch–carry quest. This involves the character being sent to deliver an item from one location to another. Sometimes the character may need to collect the item first instead of being handed the item to deliver when starting the quest. These quests are made challenging by asking the character to journey through unfamiliar or dangerous terrain, sometimes while facing a time limit.

Gather quests

Gather quests, also known as collection quests, require a character to collect a number of items. These can either be gathered from a location or environment, or require the character to kill creatures in order to collect the required items. The quest may also require the character to collect a number of different items, for example, to assemble a device.

Escort quests

The *escort quest* involves slaying monsters to maintain the well-being of a non-player character (NPC). A typical escort quest would involve protecting the NPC character as he or she moves through a monster-infested area. A majority of the time the quest will require the player to slay multiple monsters to ensure the safety of the NPC…

Hybrids

Elements from the above types can be combined to make more complex quests. For example, a quest could require that the player find the parts needed to assemble a specific weapon (Gather quest) and then use it to kill a specific foe (Kill quest). Hybrid quests may also include puzzles and riddles.

Quest chains

A *quest chain* is a group of quests that are completed in sequence… Completion of each quest is necessary before beginning the next quest in the chain. Quests usually increase in difficulty as a player progresses through the chain. Quest chains often start with small tasks in order to encourage characters to journey to a new place, where further elements of the quest chain are revealed…

Adapted from **https://en.wikipedia.org/wiki/Quest_(video_gaming)**

You will be assessed using the following criteria.

Criterion B: Comprehending written and visual text (Text handling)

3Bi *Show understanding of information, main ideas and supporting details, and draw conclusions*

3Bii *Understand basic conventions including aspects of format and style, and author's purpose for writing*

3Biii *Engage with the written and visual text by identifying ideas, opinions and attitudes and by making a response to the text based on personal experiences and opinions*

Criterion C: Communicating in response to spoken and/or written and/or visual text

3Ci *Respond appropriately to spoken and/or written and/or visual text*

3Cii *Interact in rehearsed and unrehearsed exchanges*

3Ciii *Express ideas and feelings, and communicate information in familiar and some unfamiliar situations*

3Civ *Communicate with a sense of audience and purpose.*

Criterion D: Using language in spoken and/or written form

3Di *Write and/or speak using a range of vocabulary, grammatical structures and conventions; when speaking, use clear pronunciation and intonation*

3Dii *Organize information and ideas and use a range of basic cohesive devices*

3Diii *Use language to suit the context*

Going beyond the chapter

In this chapter you have explored quest stories. As a result we can examine the relationships between individuals and the societies in which they live from personal, local and global perspectives. Now make use of the information you have learned and the communication skills you have developed in this chapter for practical purposes beyond the classroom.

Take action! Some suggestions ...

Short play

Use the drama skills you have developed in this chapter to write and produce a short performance about the personal quest of someone you personally admire. You may want to concentrate on two or three key scenes in that person's quest.

Research the lives of one or two people who have to make a choice either to stay behind or follow their heart. Such people often have to embark on a difficult or risky journey, or undertake a difficult task. You could link this activity to someone you have learned about in Individuals and Societies or another subject.

Alternatively, find out about a member of your family, or one of your circle of friends or neighbours who has gone on some form of quest. That person may have undertaken a difficult journey such as emigrating from one country to another. Alternatively, the quest may have been more personal, such as a love story.

You could delve deeper into the character of this person by exploring their motivations and actions, or the context in which the action takes place.

Once you are ready, create your dialogue, rehearse and then act out your drama. You can record the final performance and show it to an invited audience.

Service learning

Speak to your MYP coordinator or action and service coordinator to find out your school's expectations for action and service in your particular grade/year.

The ideas below relate directly to the following service learning outcomes:

- undertake challenges that develop new skills

- persevere in action

- work collaboratively with others

- develop international-mindedness through global engagement, multilingualism and intercultural understanding.

Ideas for service

Drama can be a very powerful tool to help others visualize and experience an important topic that you want to publicize. Drama can capture an audience's attention and can be more effective and more direct than creating a poster or delivering a speech about a topic.

You could use your drama skills and understanding of the topic of quests to write and present a drama on one of the following issues that relate to this theme:

- refugees

- migrant workers

- a quest for justice

- a quest for equality (human rights, gender issues, access to education).

Alternatively, you may want to dramatize a related topic of your own choosing.

You could use a drama to inspire others to join your service activity or to support a specific initiative in which one group seeks to help another.

Create a drama showing how someone accepted a challenge to make a difference. You could ask to perform your drama piece in a school assembly or as part of a fundraising or awareness creation event.

If you enjoyed this chapter here are some texts for further reading

C.S. Lewis, *The Lion, the Witch and the Wardrobe*

Rodman Philbrick, *Freak the Mighty*

Rodman Philbrick, *Max the Mighty*

Rick Riordan, *The Percy Jackson* series

"Star Wars" books

J.R.R. Tolkien, *The Hobbit*

ATL Research and thinking skills

At the end of any learning experience always ask yourself these questions:

- What lessons have I learned from this chapter?
- What concepts don't I yet understand about this topic?
- What questions do I still have about this topic?
- Where can I find answers to these questions?